My Life Adds Up

A Memoir

By

Frederick S. Hillhouse

My Life Adds Up
A Memoir

ISBN-13: 978-154840789
ISBN-10: 1548404780

Author: Frederick S. Hillhouse

For permission, please contact:
David S. Larson
davidslarson@yahoo.com

Printed as a work of non-fiction in the U.S.A.

Editing and layout by David Larson.

Cover Design by Kari Cureton.

DEDICATION

To My Loving Family

John Thomas Hillhouse, brother

Helen Simmons Hillhouse, mother of Susan and Sara

Niece Susan Hillhouse Beach and
her husband Guy Kay Beach

Niece Sara Hillhouse Sallembien and
Husband Francois Lucien Sallembien
Their children:
William Andrew Jean Sallembien
Henry Michel Frederick Sallembien
Joseph Francois Maurice Sallembien
James Hillhouse Sallembien
Eliza Mary Bradford Sallembien

Forever Loved Deceased Family

Helen Howard Sisson, grandmother

Andrew Fitch Hillhouse, Sr., father
Ednah Beatrice Sisson, mother

Ruth Sisson Lamb, aunt

Andrew Fitch Hillhouse, Jr., brother

Nancy Hillhouse, sister

Brandon James Beach, grand-nephew

1

I count, add, and tabulate. I sort, catalogue, and file. That's what I've done most of my life as a bookkeeper. Debits and credits. Ledgers and balances. In my home, there are walls of custom cupboards filled with neatly labeled boxes, and file cabinets containing folders and binders with tabs listing the documents that are the substance of my life. They all certify, with precise correctness, where I've been, what I've done, and that I existed in this world. For me, there is a profound comfort in this order.

My name is Frederick Sisson Hillhouse and I have lived a full life. I am 95 years old and reside in Point Loma, originally a Portuguese fishing village far west of San Diego that juts out into the endless blue Pacific Ocean. I never married and have no children, but I have a love of life that's boundless.

My life's story has added up to what you're about to read.

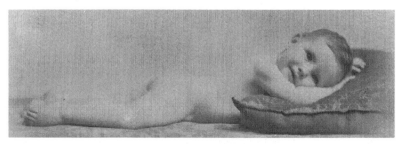

Nine months old in 1922. My only nude picture (hope you don't mind)

I was born November 5, 1921, in the Passaic General Hospital in New Jersey at a cost for delivery of only $20.00.

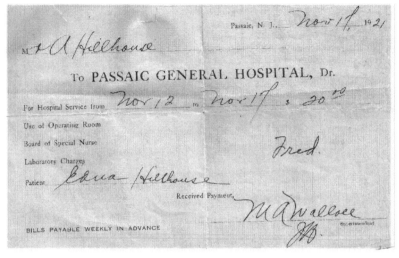

My first memory comes from when I was five, tugging my red Radio Flyer wagon, loaded with my mother Ednah's magazines—*Time, Life, Better Homes & Gardens,* and *Harper's Bazaar.* I walked up and down the sidewalks of our Pittsburgh, Pennsylvania neighborhood, from house to house, up long brick sidewalks lined with perfectly-trimmed plants, to ring door buzzers and repeat the speech my mother rehearsed with me. I didn't understand half her words, but at least I could pronounce them.

At many of the homes, I had to stand on a pile of magazines to reach the buzzer, my dark brown polished leather shoes on their tiptoes. When the door opened, I bowed slightly and doffed my small gray cap. "Good afternoon, ma'am. My name is Frederick Sisson Hillhouse of eight hundred Fisher Street. I have a wonderful selection of magazines," my small arm waved back at my wagon, "in excellent condition and at half the newsstand price, only five cents each. Would you like to peruse any of them?"

The lady of the house or their maids would always give a warm smile and come out to take a look. If it was a cold winter day, they'd invite in for a cup of hot cocoa. But no matter what, they usually gave me a nickel. When I returned home, I dumped the change on the kitchen table. Something about coins bouncing on hard wood always brings me back to that time. I counted each nickel and stacked them in piles of five, then took out my pencil and marked the total in a small notebook, tallying up my take.

"How much this time, Frederick?" my mother asked, always seeming to be standing at the sink fussing with something or directing our maid how to properly peel a carrot.

We didn't need the money. My dad had a good job that provided us with a big house, a maid, and he had a company car that kept him on the road for much of the time. Somehow my mother knew I'd enjoy the activity.

I looked to my notebook and ran my nickel-stained index finger to the latest entry. "Uh, one dollar and fifteen cents."

"That's wonderful. Now, what's your total?" She placed her hands on her hips and gave me a big smile.

I knew she was going to ask, and I was ready. "Twelve dollars and fifty-seven cents."

"Are you sure that's right? Where'd the extra two cents come from?"

"I sold Mrs. Thorndike three magazines for twelve cents last week."

"Oh, that's right." She walked over to me and placed her hand on my shoulder, then turned to look back out the kitchen window, the small yellow curtains parted just enough to see the weather. "You're going to go places, Frederick. I wish Andy was as industrious. All he seems to want to do is plays sports all day, just like your father when he was young." She leaned down and kissed my forehead. Scents of warm talcum powder and starched cotton filled my nose.

She broke away to pull down the blue and orange Maxwell House Coffee tin from atop our new Frigidaire. I slid the small stacks of nickels off the table and into the tin. I hefted it in my hands—it was getting heavy.

"Now, off to wash your hands, Frederick."

That day, in an odd kind of way, my future was cast for me. I would become a bookkeeper, a position that would take me from shore to shore across America for five decades. It would barely feed my three growing passions—live theater, ballroom dancing, and beer.

2

Hillhouse is my family name and I'm proud of it. All my life, I heard family stories of our heritage going back to the start of the American colonies. After I got out of the Navy in 1946 at the age of twenty-five, I decided to find out for myself. Maybe it was something about our country surviving a world war that set things in motion for me—but I'll get to that later.

My first stop was the New York Public Library in Manhattan. There, with the help of a librarian and the Dewey Decimal System, I discovered a tome by a Reverend James Hillhouse which listed the genealogy of the Hillhouse name, mostly taken from the front pages of old Bibles. The task of tracking down so many names overwhelmed me. At the same time, I could feel time marching forward without me, an urgency almost in the air following the war. The Ink Spots' *To Each His Own* seemed to be playing everywhere I went, and the lyrics tugged at me. I needed a job. I set aside my quest, promising to return to it another day.

I did –fifty years later.

During my forced retirement in 1997, I reopened this door to my past. It took me two years to gather the paperwork and have it notarized. In 1999, at the age of 78, I was granted membership in the Mayflower Society in 1999, as a tenth-generation descendant of the original settlers. Earlier, I applied for, and received, membership in the Sons of Colonial New England, and the Sons of the American Revolution 1983. I don't participate in any of their goings-on, but I framed each of their certificates and cherish them—something I hope to pass along to my relatives.

The following is some of what I discovered.

Ten generations before I was born, my great-great-great-great-something grandfather, 30-year-old William Bradford stepped foot off the Mayflower onto Plimouth, Massachusetts ("Plimouth" was the original spelling). On November 9, 1620, he began a journal that would span his thirty-one years in the colony and become the premiere document for future historians to understand early colonists' lives. He also became the first governor of the settlement, a position he held for thirty-one years.

William Bradford's life was not without sorrow. During his voyage to America on the Mayflower, his wife, Dorothy Wiswall Bradford, fell overboard and drowned. Mystery and scandal surrounds the sad event. One story suggests she had an affair with Christopher Jones, the ship's 50-year-old captain, and that God punished her for her adultery.

Nonetheless, William Bradford remarried a year after arrival in Plymouth. Alice Bradford bore him a son and daughter, Joseph and Mercy, joining sons William Jr. and John as his children from his previous wife.

William Bradford held the position of Governor and chief magistrate in Plymouth, acting as high judge and treasurer, as well as presiding over the deliberations of the General Court, the legislature of the community. From everything I read, he appeared to be an honorable and fair man. As such, in 1636, he helped draft the colony's legal code.

Under his guidance, Plymouth never became a Bible commonwealth like its larger and more influential neighbor, the Massachusetts Bay Colony. Rather, Plymouth settlers did not restrict the franchise or other civic privileges to church members. Their churches were Congregationalist and Separatist in form, yet Presbyterians like William Vassal resided in the colony without being pressured to conform to the majority's religious convictions.

After a brief experiment with the "common course," a sort of primitive farming communism, the colony quickly centered on private subsistence agriculture. This was facilitated by Bradford's decision to distribute land among all the settlers, not just members of the company.

On my mother's Sisson side, I am a descendant of Charlemagne. He was also known as the "Father of Europe," or Charles I, King of the Franks (France) from 800-814. Being a 36th generation relative of such royalty is of interest to me and a source of some pride.

Aside from the smile, notice any resemblance?

These are my roots, not that I clung to them much during my life. Had I known more of my family's deep history at the time, I might have made different choices—got a college degree, found someone and fell in love. But isn't that what life is all about, the choices we make and the paths we take?

3

My grandmother, "Nana" to me and my siblings, lived with us until her death. She was the main "cook and babysitter" and always made delicious deserts. She was the kind of grandma who would lay down the law, but just as quick give you a hug. Knowing how hungry boys can be, especially for sweets, when she'd bake a cake, after we had a slice after dinner, she'd take the remainder and hide it under her bed. That Andy and I knew about it, tells you how conniving we could be—and how nice Nana was to us. But we never dared stealing a piece.

1923 at New Jersey Shore
Father on the left, me next to him, Andy ahead of me

* * *

When I turned eight years old, Mother decided to sign me up for lessons in a variety of activities. "Every young man needs a sense of culture and grace, Frederick," she reminded me, before I was handed off to another instructor. Archery. Tap dance. Piano. Golf. My closet began to fill with the remnants of failed sports and art.

At the time, we were 30 years away from television, the first radio station in Pittsburgh didn't broadcast until 1920, a year before I was born, so *activities* were what it was all about for children of upper middle-class America. I forget which I first took, but only one stuck—ballroom dancing.

I practiced piano lessons Saturday mornings at our home with Daniel Moss, the father of one of my dad's A&P employees. Since I wasn't interested in doing scales, that didn't last.

Golf was only a frustration for my gangly ever-growing body. I overheard the golf pro from the club tell my mother, "I don't get it. His older brother, Andy, has all the makings of a great player. Mrs. Hillhouse, if I continue on with Frederick, I'm afraid I'll just be wasting your money."

My mother looked at me with disappointed eyes as I held a club against my shoulder like it was a rifle, aiming at imaginary birds flying overhead. No more golf.

I took tap dance lessons from Mrs. Grammercy in the parlor of her home. To this day, the smell of gardenias or lemon oil reminds me of her forever-pinched frown as she clapped out the beat to Al Jolson singing *Toot Toot Tootsie, Goodbye* on her gramophone. Tap lasted three weeks.

My brother Andy was great at basketball, golf, football—actually, any sport. He definitely was the jock in our family, taking after our Dad. He took violin lessons. Finally, something he wasn't so accomplished at. My only saving grace was that we didn't share a room, but I could hear the banshees from his violin strings wailing from his across the hall.

One of the few things Andy and I had in common—our tonsils were removed on the same day, September 1, 1928, by the same physician, Dr. C.E. Fawcett. We shared ice cream and Jell-O during our one-week recovery—his tonsillectomy taking, but not mine. Three years later, when I was ten, I went through the ordeal again, but this time alone. And the cost for our double-tonsillectomy back then? Only $55 each.

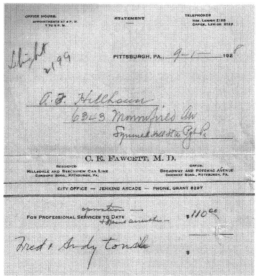

The Doctor's Bill for two Tonsillectomies

12

MY LIFE ADDS UP

Every August, before school started up, my mother took us clothes shopping. Lord & Taylor put together a traveling caravan of fashion that showed up each year in local hotels— taking over a hotel room with racks and such to displays their clothes. Mother got us completely outfitted. For her, it was efficient, the clothes were classic, and she could stop worrying about it for the rest of the year.

Although the Great Depression was going on, I never felt it. Dad's job was secure because people still needed to eat and he kept receiving promotions to oversee more A&P stores located in the upper mid-west to the northeast. Cleveland. Pittsburgh. Utica. Syracuse. Buffalo. The towns we moved to became a blur, the schools and teachers nothing but jumbled memories. If I didn't still have my class photos, I wouldn't remember attending those schools.

I was always good at math. In the 4th grade, my teacher appointed me to be in charge of collecting the deposits of my classmates, kind of like a mini-bank to teach them to save— mostly pennies and nickels, a few dimes. Next to each name I wrote down the exact amount of their deposits. Today you'd call it a Christmas account. She deposited everything in a single account at the bank. At the end of the year, she brought back all the money and I helped her give it back to the students—with interest. When we were finished, she patted me on the back. At that point in my life, it was the most satisfaction I got out of doing anything—and I felt important.

Math came easy for me. If there was a row of numbers on a chalkboard, I'd be the first in class with my hand up—and my answers were always right. After a while, teachers stopped calling on me, satisfied with embarrassing some other kid in my class.

One constant through all that upheaval and change was Mother's insistence on exploring life's opportunities. "Expand your horizons, Frederick. There's so much the world has to offer. Give everything a chance."

* * *

In 7th grade at John F. Hughes School, my homeroom and English teacher was Mr. Moore. He gave us a book report as an assignment, with a month to complete it. Since my reading material at the time was comic books, Sunday funnies, *Life* and *Look* magazines, and the *National Geographic* (for the pictures), I was ill-prepared and disinterested in wading through a lengthy book just to write a stupid paper.

I stared at *Mary Poppins* sitting on my night stand every night before going to bed, but just couldn't get myself to open the cover. Mr. Moore's voice kept nagging me as the deadline drew near. "No more than two pages, and in your best penmanship. This book report will go a long way to your grade for the year, so put some thought into it."

Sunday, the day before the paper was due, we had just come back from Baptist Sunday School, and I was immersed in the funnies. I spotted a book review for *Mary Poppins* in the paper. What luck and providence. I cut out the article and late that night, took bits and pieces to write the best book report Mr. Moore ever saw—even my penmanship sparkled. I was convinced I'd get an A.

Late that week, when Mr. Moore passed out our grades, he called me up to the front of the room. He held up my paper, I was sure to let all my fellow students know what an incredible book report I crafted—such deep insights, perfect penmanship, and so concise.

Instead, he announced, "This is what you do NOT do in my class."

My mouth hung open and I looked around for friendly faces, but only received cold stares.

He continued, "It seems Fred would rather plagiarize than read a book and write a report, like all you other students." He pulled out a copy of the newspaper review—and my heart sank. He placed his hand on my shoulder and looked me in the eye. "I'm certain Fred will enjoy the special assignment I have for him."

For the next four months of the school year, I read a book a month and wrote book reports which I read aloud to the class. That was the last time I ever plagiarized anyone. I managed to get a C for that class, pretty much like all the other C's I received in all my other subjects.

* * *

Ballroom dance lessons at the Steele Sisters' home is where I discovered my first passion at the age of thirteen. I enjoyed it so much, I always made certain our maid gave my pants and dress shirt a crisp ironing. I stopped in front of our hallway mirror to check that everything was in place, my dark brown hair parted neatly to the left, my belt lined up with my shirt buttons, my sweater tied around my neck, my two-tone brogues clean. A nod to myself, and I was out our front door and into my mother's maroon LaSalle joining my older brother Andy.

Ten minutes later, we dashed up the sidewalk to the Steele's stately two-story white home, but slowed down before we got to the steps to compose ourselves. Two sharp raps on the front door and Julie, the elder of the two twenty-ish, brown-haired sisters, welcomed our feet onto the slick sheen of the oak floor in the large entryway where we danced.

"How nice to see you again, Andy and Fred."

"You too, as well, Miss Steele," we answered in unison.

As the door closed, I heard Mother pull away from the curb, certain her sons were in the capable hands of good women who would teach us what's right about the world. The Steele Sisters always stood with one foot slightly lifted off the heel and pointed outward, their chins raised as if they were willing their necks to be longer, forever poised for imaginary photographers. I was in awe of them.

"Your frame," Julie reminded the six boys and six girls at the start of each lesson, "is the most important aspect of proper ballroom dance." She eyed us over as we stood with our arms frozen in space as if we were holding an invisible partner—usually picking on me to make a slight adjustment by lifting one of my hands or turning my wrist. "Without a good frame, you might as well try driving a car without a steering wheel."

She waited until we answered as a group, "Yes, Miss Steele."

"A girl needs to feel secure and safe on the dance floor," Patricia, the younger Steele sister, admonished the boys, her head shaking slowly from side to side. "Refrain from pressing your face or body against her. That is employed by boorish types who have no respect for their dance partners, or themselves. Remember, decorum and modesty are to be adhered to at all times."

"For those of you who came here to learn the Charleston or the Jitterbug, we will attend to those in later lessons." Julie put her hands on her hips. "Know this, you will find plenty of up-tempo music for ballroom dance that will fill you with high spirits and transport you to a world of elegance and charm." She gazed past us out the large plate glass living room window, as if lost in hopes of days, and men, who awaited her.

"Go ahead now and take a partner," Patricia said, taking over.

At six-feet tall, I towered over most of my classmates, only two inches more to grow into my final height. I usually selected Deborah. She was the tallest girl in the class and always wore white with a pink ribbon in her blonde hair. I sneaked looks at us in the hall mirror and continually straightened my back to the posture the Steele Sisters insisted we maintain.

The best part was the way girls smelled. Just close enough to notice their freshness, with a hint of nervous, like me. Then there was the way they felt, taking her right hand in my left, my right hand cupping her shoulder. I moved her across the floor in my frame, trying to keep to the beat of the music while not stepping on her feet, or bumping into someone, or looking her in the eyes. Definitely the most exhilarating and frightening moments in my life—and I loved it.

Those years of ballroom dance lessons would serve me well to meet girls, and women. They guided me all through my high school years in a fraternity, my brief stay in college, my time in the Navy during WWII, and long after in nightclubs from New York to San Francisco.

Junior High School Graduating Class. I'm the one without the tie!

4

My brush with religion came from when my parents would drop me and my siblings off at the Tabernacle Baptist Church each Sunday morning and pick us up following services. I secretly guessed they wanted some time alone. I was baptized on April 14, 1933, when I was eleven years old, so I guess I'm a Baptist. You wouldn't know it by how many times I attended church in my life—aside from friends' weddings or funerals.

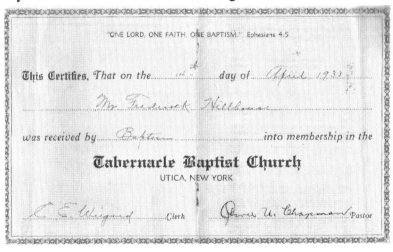

* * *

My Nana introduced me to the world of live theater when I was 15 years old. We were living in Utica at the time and she got tickets for me to go with her to see George M. Cohan's one-man show *Dear Old Darling*. I didn't care that it was January 25, 1936, in the dead of winter. The music, the dancing, the singing—I was enthralled—so much so, I saved the program.

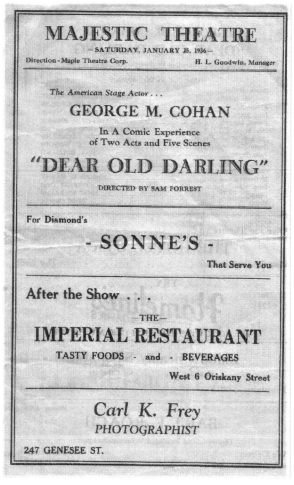

* * *

I disliked everything about school. John F. Hughes Grade School. Utica Free Academy High School (UFA). The Bentley School of Accounting in Boston. The classes, studying, and tests were nothing but misery to me. My grades bounced between respectable B's and C's—just enough to get by. I'm amazed I graduated high school, coming in 466th out of 504 students.

My favorite family home in Utica

The only good thing about high school was the social life. I joined the Phi Delta Sigma Fraternity at fourteen when I started at UFA, my brother signing up the year before. I made it through initiation by laying on a cold basement floor blindfolded, swallowing a raw egg, eating a clove of garlic, and getting paddled by a gauntlet of teenage boys—my backside sore for a week—my brother meting out the hardest blow.

The fraternity gathered monthly at one of the members' homes, usually in their basement. Before the meetings officially came to order, a group of boys huddled in a corner shooting dice. Since gambling was of no interest to me, I never participated. Meetings involved collecting five dollar-a-month dues, deciding on new members, and planning events. That's what we were most famous for, the dances, where we invited a local sorority or two to join us.

For our Christmas holiday parties, we hired some of the biggest bands around. One year we had singer Ella Fitzgerald with drummer Chick Webb and his band. Her hit a *Tisket a Tasket* had us jumping all over the dance floor. Fletcher Henderson with his band headlined another Christmas party. These were formal affairs, black tie or tails. The music was the best. The girls looked their best. Everyone danced their best.

Ella Fitzgerald with Chick Webb on drums

* * *

A week after my 16th birthday, Dad took me out in our maroon LaSalle to teach me to drive. In many ways, he was more nervous than I was, filling the ashtray with cigarette after cigarette, barking out commands. "Turn. Not right, left. No, stop here. Now, back up slowly."

By the time I drove up our driveway, I had enough. When I turned too sharply into the garage, I put a three-foot scrape in the drivers' side of his car. That was the last lesson Dad gave me.

In fact, the next time I drove anything would be 26 years later when I was 42, living in San Francisco, where my "ride" was a light blue Lambretta Scooter.

* * *

Both of my parents were athletic. Father played football in college as well as other sports, and Mother was a golfer. I accompanied her as her caddy one summer when I was 15 while we were vacationing at Brantingham Lake, New York—at a cabin tucked away in the Adirondacks. On one of the Par-3 holes, we probably spent 10 minutes looking for her ball. That was, until I looked in the cup! She got a hole-in-one! She and Father celebrated afterwards at the clubhouse's 19th hole.

* * *

I like a good joke, but was never known for pulling pranks. A harmless one from high school shows you why. On warm nights, a few of my friends would join me for a walk "up the hill" to Hamilton College and serenade the students in their ivy-covered brick dorm buildings from the grassy quad below. For all we knew, no one ever heard us—we were never chased from the campus by security and no students ever poked their heads out of their dorm windows. Our favorite rehearsed song was *Hold Tight*. The lyrics will show you why we weren't any threat to anyone who might be listening.

Hold tight, hold tight, hold tight, hold tight
Foo-ra-de-ack-a-sa-ki
Want some seafood Mama
Shrimpers and rice they're very nice
Hold tight, hold tight, hold tight, hold tight
Foo-ra-de-ack-a-sa-ki
Want some seafood Mama
Steamers and sauce and then of course I like oysters lobsters too
And I like my tasty butter fish
When I come home from work at night
I get my favorite dish, fish!
Hold tight, hold tight, hold tight, hold tight
Foo-ra-de-ack-a-sa-ki
Want some seafood Mama

* * *

I believe I mentioned that we always had a maid to help clean around the house, with the four children, wash clothes, iron, run errands, and help Nana in our kitchen. The summer of 1938, Dad rented a cottage on Oneida Lake, and as always, Nana and our maid, Mary, came along. I ended up dating Sharon, a girl who lived in a cottage nearby. Her father was a captain of a banana boat. Well, he found his way over to our place and took a liking to Mary. Looking back, it sounds odd, but I double-dated with his daughter, and him with Mary. It was fine by me!

* * *

On Saturday, November 12, 1938, when I was 17, Robert Sherman, my best friend at the time, invited me to join him and his parents for a night on Broadway at the Imperial Theater in New York City. We took the train in and had dinner at a Chinese restaurant around the corner from the Imperial. Everything about the night was spectacular—starting with the sweet and sour pork.

Cole Porter composed the words and music for his musical *Leave it to Me*, and the all-star cast that night included Sophie Tucker, William Gaxton, and Victor Moore. Much like me seeing my first live performance, making her Broadway debut was Mary Martin. We sat in the last row of the orchestra. She jumped up on a steamer trunk at a railway station, did a bit of a striptease, and sang *My Heart Belongs to Daddy*. That was it for me.

Not only did that performance launch her career, but everything about the production got me tapping my feet and filled my heart with wonder. Mary Martin would go on to a glorious career, winning a Tony Award in 1946 for her role as Nurse Nellie Forbush in Rogers & Hammerstein's *South Pacific*.

With Bob Sherman at local lake camp

You might wonder why I know all this—I should. I've seen hundreds of musicals and plays during my life. The last time I was in New York, I took in 16 live theater performances in two weeks. As you might expect, I did the math—532 musicals and plays over 77 years, that's nearly seven per year. If it weren't for WWII and my time living away from big cities, I probably would have doubled that. There's just something about live theater with love stories told through song, that takes me to a place like no other.

* * *

I didn't mention before, but I dated Margarite Cullen for my four high school years. She had dark hair, down to her shoulders, and a dazzling smile. Lots of kissing and canoodling, but no hanky-panky with her.

When I was in the Navy, I kept this photo of her on my desk while I was in pharmacy school. I corresponded with her every week, but each letter she wrote me felt like she was getting further and further away. I received a final letter from her when I was in San Francisco, just before heading to the Pacific Theater—she married a man who owned a dairy farm. That broke my heart a little.

* * *

We often would vacation at Lake Oneida during summers, and between my junior and senior years, we spent a few weeks. We'd often go to the club and listen to whatever band was playing, and there were some good ones.

Glenn Miller and he orchestra were playing and during the break, our dates went to powder their noses while we went to the bar. Who should we find but Benny Goodman. We have a delightful chat within until our dates arrived. One of them asked, "Who is he?"

He leaned over and whispered to me, "You ought to find other dates. These are pretty blasé."

* * *

My one moment of fame came during my senior year. As a member of the Drama Club, I was cast as Sheridan Whiteside in the play, *The Man Who Came to Dinner*. I was in one scene, in a wheelchair, wearing a smoking jacket with a long cigarette holder in my hand. I had many lines, but one that would get a huge laugh—it did during rehearsals. Somehow, amidst all the backstage lights and queues and wardrobe, when I finally arrived on the stage to deliver that line ... I forgot it. The line, which is seared into my memory now is: "Miss Bed Pan, where are you?"

Ta-da!

* * *

My graduation from Utica Free Academy High School on June 26, 1940, was without fanfare. In fact, the following summer months were nothing but lounging by pools, going to dances, and sneaking sherry from my parents' liquor cabinet.

Our home became a haven for me and my friends with the sunroom's ping-pong table, a juke box, and pinball machine. Out in the back yard, we used to play badminton and horseshoes for hours.

Since I didn't sign up for college, I took a job, my first job, at the urging of Dad. On the corner of Genesee and Bleeker Streets stood The Boston Store. I worked in the Men's Department for thirty cents an hour, the minimum wage. I was paid to fold and hang dress shirts and ties, boxers and socks, for both display and selling to customers. At that time, boxer shorts sold for 8¢ and long johns for 50¢. To help select the right size, I held them up in front of a customer. Two good things came from all of that—my clothes in my closet at home, as well as my dresser, never looked so neat and organized—and my wardrobe grew.

My new clothes came in handy for going out with my three best friends for dancing, bars, and live theater. We met lots of ladies out on the town, but I always showed them respect—the words of the Steele sisters ringing in my ears, reminding me the proper way to frame when dancing and how uncouth it was to be a boor, or worse yet, a womanizer.

* * *

We had a fire. Had my youngest brother John not smelled it in the middle of the night and alerted everyone, who knows what would have happened. Apparently, some wires under a rug frayed, setting a small blaze. After the volunteer fireman put out the fire, Mother asked them in for drinks. Always the hostess.

5

In the spring of 1941, Dad pressed me, "Working at the Boston Store isn't taking you anywhere, Frederick. You can't just idle your life away. It's time to make something of yourself—get an education, start a career."

I tossed around the idea of heading to the Wharton School of Business—but the intensity of their academic life didn't appeal to me. Maybe it was my older brother Andy attending MIT in Cambridge, Massachusetts, that got me thinking of schools in that area.

"You were always good with numbers," Mother said to me as I filled out the forms to attend the Bentley School of Accounting and Finance in Boston.

I was accepted and started my freshman year in September 1941, taking up residence a few blocks away from the school. I well remember the first Fall day of school, looking up at the four-story brick building on Boylston Street, promising to apply myself and do well.

Like it was in grade school and high school, I quickly lost interest in classes, studying, homework, and tests. Instead, I attended every live theater performance, vaudeville show, and movie there was to see in Boston. Finding good dance spots was next on my list, and with Dad footing the bill for my education, my first year was happy and secured.

Bentley School of Accounting and Finance, Boston

Three months in, as you well know, on December 7, 1941, the Japs attacked Pearl Harbor. I heard the news at supper time that Sunday. After that, every radio and newspaper relived the "day of infamy." Right away, students dropped out of school and enlisted. I could almost smell the urgency and desperation in the air—but it didn't seem to take hold of me.

I brought it up to my brother Andy when he drove us both home at Christmas in his dark green 1936 Ford Phaeton convertible. "You're in your third year at MIT, Andy. What are you going to do about the war?"

"Keep going to school. What about you, Fred?"

"The same, I guess."

Talk around the dinner table during the holidays was kept civil with my twelve-year-old brother John Thomas and my baby sister Nancy in attendance. Around the neighborhood though, and everywhere I'd go, the war was all everyone mentioned.

Back in Boston, to pick up some extra spending cash for all the entertainment I wanted, I worked as a nanny for Billy Hubbard, an eight-year-old boy from a military family. After getting out of class, I'd pick him up from his home and we'd walk to the Esplanade long the Charles River where we'd give all the playground equipment a workout.

* * *

I didn't give up completely of my love of the theater while away I was at college. In one encounter, orchestra ticket holders had the option to walk down the aisle and onto the stage where we could meet some of the cast, then go back to our seats. And who did I get to meet? None other than Carmen Miranda!

*   *   *

The Hollywood Victory Caravan train tour rolled into Boston on May 1, 1942. Bob Hope and Cary Grant were the emcees, and the stars were never any better. For three-and-a-half hours, Bing Crosby sang, James Cagney danced and sang patriotic George M. Cohan's songs, and Laurel and Hardy did their famous Driver's License sketch. Movie stars Claudette Colbert, Merle Oberon, Joan Bennett, and Joan Blondell performed as well. It was one of the biggest hoots I ever had, getting my fill of all the entertainers I loved so much.

* * *

When school let out in May 1942, I headed home somewhat embarrassed, having flunked out of the Bentley School of Accounting and Finance. At the beginning of the summer, maybe it was the way I kept asking for an increase in my allowance, Dad approached me.

"If school's not your cup of tea, Frederick, then it's time you got a job."

Why? I'm having a good time.

"There's a war on. People have to contribute somehow," he added.

I volunteered to be a member of the Ground Observer Corp in our area. Three nights a week, I'd take a thermos of Coke and a pair of binoculars, and hike to the top of a small hill a mile from my home. If I spotted any German or Japanese aircraft during my eight pm-midnight shift, I was to run to the house next door and use their telephone to call in my sighting. If my report could be verified, it would then be relayed to the Aircraft Warning Service.

I never ran next door.

* * *

For my second job ever, I drilled carbine gun barrels at the Savage Arms Munitions Factory. What a mess. To this day, the smell of hot oil and grease takes me back there. During my shift, I watched the constant flow of heavy machine oil wash over barrels as diamond-tipped drills bored into hardened steel, screaming out with each turn of the wheel. After the first day, I shoved cotton balls in my ears to help muffle the incessant noise.

Everything about the job was thick, and black, and slippery. The heavy oil-skin apron I wore couldn't keep the sludge off of me—a heavy rash on my thighs developed. Even the lunch room was soiled. That's where I'd washed my hands three times just to get them clean enough to eat the peanut butter and jelly sandwiches Mother packed for me.

On October 8, 1942, I was almost happy when I got my notice from the draft board. "Greetings: Having submitted yourself to a local board composed of your neighbors for the purpose of determining your availability for training and service in the armed forces of the United States, you are hereby notified..."

My number came up. It was time to join the Army.

My last day at Savage Arms, I looked at each gun barrel differently. I now envisioned them attached to the firing mechanisms assembled in another part of the plant, the stocks screwed on—and I imagined the carbine in the hands of a soldier overseas. A soldier who would either fight the Nazis or the Japs. A soldier who could be me.

NOTICE OF CLASSIFICATION

Registrant .... Order No. 10,833.

has been classified in Class ...1A... (Until ...., 19.....)
by ☒ Local Board   (Insert Date for Class II-A and II-B only)
     ☐ Board of Appeal (by vote of .... to ....)
     ☐ President

SEP 24 '42 ...., 19.....   F. J. Bradley Jr.
(Date of mailing)   Member of Local Board.

NOTICE OF RIGHT TO APPEAL

Appeal from classification by local board or board of appeal must be made by signing appeal form on back of questionnaire at office of local board, or by filing written notice of appeal, within ten days after the mailing of this notice.
   Before appeal, a registrant may file a written request for appearance within the same ten-day period; and, if he does so, the local board will fix a day and notify him to appear personally before the local board; if this is done, the time to appeal is extended to ten days beyond the day set by the local board for such appearance.
   There is a right in certain dependency cases, of appeal from appeal board decision to the President; see Selective Service Regulations.
The law requires you—To keep in touch with your local board.   To notify it of any change of address.
                      To notify it of any fact which might change classification.
D. S. S. Form 57 (Rev. 4-13-42)   16—19071-1   U. S. GOVERNMENT PRINTING OFFICE

On Tuesday, October 13, 1942, four weeks before my twenty-first birthday, instead of reporting to the Army, I enlisted in the Navy. Anchors aweigh!

6

Mother drove me to the US Navy Reserve Station in Utica, NY, on a cool Tuesday morning, October 13th, 1942. I spotted a huge poster in the window as she pulled up—and couldn't help but wonder what I'd be doing.

We were not a hugging-type of family. Mother simply said, "You take care of yourself, Frederick," and patted me on the shoulder.

"Sure. I'll let you know where I land."

With that, I walked in the door and was greeted by a captain with gleaming teeth in a crisp white uniform full of colored ribbons. After filling out paperwork, me and fifty other recruits boarded a bus to the US Naval Training Station in Newport, Rhode Island. First thing off the bus, we were lead single file for medical exams. I felt like a heifer at a county fair the way I was poked and prodded for the next few hours, some of it humiliating. I still have my medical records from that day.

Serial number: 600-85-71

Religion: Protestant

Complexion: Ruddy (probably from my going-away party the night before with my buddies)

Height: 6'2¼"

Weight: 162 lbs.

Eyes: Brown

Hair. Dark Brown

BP: 124/78

All else "normal."

By far, the worst day of boot camp was the first 24 hours. At the end of our medical exam, before we were issued our clothing, bedding, and sea bag, we were given a buzz haircut, and inoculated. Three shots in my left arm, two in my right. Guys all around me were passing out. Tetanus, typhus, typhoid, cholera, and the fifth shot I don't remember, and don't want to.

Someone in line with ROTC training mumbled, "They don't know where they're sending us, so they're giving us everything. You know, be prepared, just like Boy Scouts."

Everyone rubbed their shoulders through mess that evening at seven o'clock. My first Navy meal was creamed chipped beef on toast, over-boiled green beans, milk, and cherry Jell-O—nothing like Mother's cooking.

Afterwards, our instructor brought us to our quarters where we stowed our gear and got everything "ship-shape." With our arms so sore from the shots, we had to work extra hard to sling our hammocks (that was our bedding) onto hooks in the walls and attempted to lift ourselves into bed.

Before lights-out, our instructor barked something about, "Revelry at oh-five-hundred, so you best hit the sack."

I was asleep in minutes. So ended the first of my 1,225 days to come in the US Navy.

* * *

How to dress, polish boots. Exercise. Mess. Drills. Prompt, efficient, and orderly. Straight off, we were taught how to tie proper knots and stand watch, apparently the two basic roles in the Navy. Jumping jacks, pushups, calisthenics, and marching got us into some semblance of shape and order. Unlike my older brother Andy, the athlete in the family, the most exercise I'd ever done was ballroom dancing—so, it took a while for me to get with it.

Speaking of drills, as Apprentice Seamen, we learned how to salute properly, close ranks, and bark out, "Aye, aye, sir!" with loud precision, no matter what we were instructed to do. If anyone in our unit faltered, we all had to do pushups.

After three weeks of rigorous monotony, I met with an assignment officer to go over my selection of what school I'd like to attend for my role in the Navy. Gunnery. Engine Room. Flight Deck. Signal Corps. My hand went down the list and landed on Cook and Baker School. "This. This one here." My thinking was simple—I'd be first in line for chow.

"Okay, Seaman. I'll get the paperwork started."

Three days later I was called back in. "Apprentice Seaman Hillhouse, welcome to your new assignment." He handed me my papers. "You'll be attending Hospital Corps School in Portsmouth, Virginia," he waved me off.

"Uh, what about Cook and Baker School, Sir?"

He looked me over with no-nonsense eyes. "Go to transportation to arrange your travel. That is all."

"Aye, aye, sir." I saluted and did my best about-face, walking out of the room not knowing what the heck lay ahead of me at the Hospital Corps School.

* * *

A day later, I reported to the Norfolk Naval Hospital in Portsmouth, Virginia, and was immediately given a pass and told to go home. "Your training won't start until December 4. Enjoy your furlough, Seaman," the administrator informed me.

It took me two days of switching trains, with a two-night stop on Wednesday, November 18, 1942, at a Young Men's Christian Association home on 34th Street in New York City. The cost for the room for two nights was only $1.80! After that, it was on to Utica. It seemed like half the passengers on the trains were soldiers, marines, or sailors. I had something in common with men I'd never met, almost like we were a part of our own kind of fraternity—and in a way we were. Slaps on the back, buying each other drinks in the diner car, exchanging news of the war and where each of us was headed—not knowing if we'd return. The threat of death creates brotherhood, and there was a lot on those trains.

When I got home, I looked up my four best friends, three of them from my high school fraternity. I spent the next month and through Thanksgiving in uniform—that got me some new respect, opened some doors, and free drinks. Bob Sherman, who took me to my first musical on Broadway when I was 17, anchored our group. Chuck Bonner, Rod Coupe, and Bob Cullen rounded it out. After lots of laughs, dances, parties, and bars, including some live theater, the month was over.

Out for drinks with brother Andy during a break in training.

On the train ride back to the Norfolk Naval Hospital, with everything so uncertain about the future, I wondered, *Will I ever make it back to Utica again?*

* * *

For the next three weeks, I studied anatomy nonstop—the classwork a grind, but I tried to be a better student than I was in high school and accounting school. I kept at it, knowing someone's life might depend on my knowledge. My twenty-first birthday passed without notice except for a few care packages from home.

I was thankful for liberty over the holidays and I commemorated my stint in the Navy on New Years' Eve, Thursday, December 31, 1942. Following a few drinks with some buddies, beer being my beverage of choice then, we wandered into a tattoo parlor down by the docks. I left an hour later and $10 poorer, a blue anchor with "USN" in the middle of it adorning my right forearm. Seventy-three years later, it looks like a blue blob on my wrinkled skin.

My studies at the Norfolk Naval Hospital ended on January 16, 1943. Then I was sent to the Naval Hospital in Jacksonville, Florida, for 12 days. More studying, this time mostly on wound care and tropical diseases. I was shipped back to the Norfolk Naval Hospital for a week before I was transferred to NTC Camp Peary, Virginia—what would become the CIA's training ground in the decades to come.

At the time, Camp Peary was the Induction Center for the Seabees ("CB" stood for Construction Battalion) of the Navy. My job for the next 20 months was to type every word spoken by Commander Gartenlaub (Dr. Charles Gartenlaub) as he reviewed x-rays. He was a small New York Jew and one of the nicest people I ever met. If I wasn't around when he analyzed x-rays, he'd use a Dictaphone and I'd transcribe it all later. I became the fastest three-fingered typist in the office.

Weekend liberty during those months consisted of heading to Washington, D.C. with two buddies from our unit, Paul August Rosenhammer and Alfred Parker—both about six foot and lean like me. We didn't go because it was the best city to have a good time, although it was incredible. We didn't go because we could share a cheap hotel room, which we did.

We went because there were three girls from Utica who lived in D.C. who waited for us. Pat, Mary, and Doris. Lovely ladies. Movies. Dancing. Dining. Drinks. We paired up right away. Paul with Pat, Doris with Alfred, and Mary with me. Lots of smooching and canoodling going on, but no hanky-panky.

In D.C. during weekend liberty
(I'm on the far left, Alfred kneeling, Paul on the far right)

44

Getting back and forth to D.C. was no small task. Oftentimes we'd take a bus from Williamsburg to Richmond and then either catch another bus or the train into D.C. Money was tight, so sometimes we hitchhiked. One time we grabbed a ride on an empty auto trailer, hanging on in the back while the open road rushed beneath us for all 108 miles, our white uniforms gray by the time we arrived. Times like those we were glad we brought along two extra uniforms. A few times while we waited for the bus in Richmond, local firemen flagged down drivers until they found someone headed to D.C., and we got a ride.

With Paul on a trip to visit him in Kansas City in 1973

On our final liberty, before we were shipped out to the Pacific Theater of War, eventually me on a transport ship,

Alfred and Paul with Marine units, we went to D.C. one last time. It was another weekend of dancing, drinking and enjoying the company of three beautiful ladies. I didn't realize how much Paul loved Pat until our ride back Sunday night on the train. For over 100 miles, he cried on my shoulder. Sad thing is, he would never see her again.

I never fell for a gal like that—but sometimes I wish I had.

7

I was shipped back to where I started almost two years before, to the Norfolk Naval Hospital in Portsmouth, Virginia. As my orders stated, I was "to receive advanced training to become a pharmacist mate." That advanced training included lots of jumping jacks, plenty of book studies—and no liberty. On Sunday, November 5, 1944, I spent my twenty-third birthday with a few buddies at a local bar where we fed the juke box every nickel we had to keep the Andrews Sisters' *Drinking Rum and Coke* playing through the night.

After a total of 10 weeks, my last day in Portsmouth was with USO gals serving me turkey, stuffing, jellied cranberry sauce, string beans, mashed potatoes, and gravy for Thanksgiving. Something about sharing a holiday meal with a bunch of sailors felt like I discovered a new family of sorts—and it felt good.

My next orders sent me to the US Naval Hospital in Pensacola, Florida, to put all my training to practical use. I was assigned to the surgical ward where wounded Marines and sailors were brought in for intensive care, many of them already bounced between two or three other hospitals before they arrived there. Double-decker bunks for sleeping, Captain's inspections of our quarters to make sure everything was ship-shape—that was the drill.

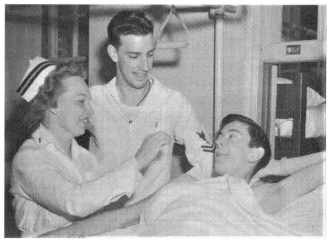

Nurse Jacobs and me with William Wilson in Pensacola

My favorite patient was William Wilson. He was also the first one I cared for every morning. His wounds from Saipan left him paralyzed from the waist down, and he had contracted huge bed sores on his spine and heels from inactivity during his previous hospital stays. No matter how bad things were, William always smiled and had a joke for me.

One I still remember, after I asked him how he was doing, he answered, "Fine as frog's hair."

"How fine is that, William?"

"So fine you can't see it."

Had his nurse, Miss Jacobs, not been such a royal pain, both his and my stay might have gone better. As it was, my job was to relieve him of his impaction every morning. For those of you who don't know what that means, when you're paralyzed from the waist down, your bowels don't function properly and they need to be evacuated manually—thus the impaction detail. Then, I treated his bed sores and made William some gauze donuts to protect the wounds from getting worse. It may all sound kind of revolting, but even I was surprised it didn't bother me.

After three months of that, I was ordered to the USNA BPD in San Bruno, California, as a staging area before heading to the Pacific. The four-day train ride across the US was monotonous, and if I wasn't sleeping, I was in the dining car at the bar. I arrived in San Bruno on Saturday, March 10, 1945.

The day before, 330 American B-29's bombers dropped incendiary bombs on Tokyo, killing 100,000 people, destroying a quarter of the city, and leaving one million Japanese homeless. To do the most damage, I heard we used something new called napalm, a gasoline-based, jelly-like substance that was created at Harvard University.

Finally, it felt like we might be winning the war. Five months later, on August 6, 1945, we would drop a hydrogen bomb on Hiroshima and that would change everything.

The Navy staging and training facility in San Bruno was on the grounds of the Tanforan Racetrack. More inoculations and sore arms, and physicals—they wanted to make sure we were all fit for duty overseas. Lots of jumping jacks, the shooting range and cleaning our carbines, and marching in close quarters for nearly a month.

The most frightening exercise was going into a gas chamber. In groups of 50, we donned our masks and were led into a large bunker. No windows, only a few overhead lights. Two sets of large steel double doors at both ends. Observing us in the room, also wearing gas masks, were training personnel.

"You will keep your masks on at all times until instructed to do otherwise," speakers blared above us.

I looked around at my shipmates, all of our masks fogging from our heavy breath, heads turning from side to side, anxious to get out of that room. Six months before, we heard of Nazi gas chambers and the thousands, if not millions, of Jews who they killed in them. I wondered what it was like for them.

A hissing from above had us all look up. A light fog began to fill the air around us. "Stay calm and breath normally," the voice from the speakers instructed.

Like me, most of us looked toward the doors, willing them to open so we could escape into the sun and fresh air. It must have only been a minute or two, but it felt like much longer, when we received our final instructions.

"Take a deep breath and take off your masks. Now, let it out and run out the doors."

Like everyone else, I waited until we saw the instructors begin to open the doors, then held my breath, took off my mask, and got the hell out of that room.

* * *

Before boarding the USS Wharton to depart San Francisco, women seated at USO tables by the dock handed each sailor a small white cotton bag with a red drawstring. Two hundred of us in our medical unit, along with 525 crew members, stepped onto the gangway of the USS Wharton on April 8th, 1945, for a three-day voyage to Seattle where we were to pick up cargo, supplies, Marines, and soldiers. Our next orders not known to the rank and file.

USS Wharton

The Wharton was an AP-7 troop transport ship, 636 feet from stem to stern. I'd sailed a few times on a friend's 22-foot sloop during summers on Long Island Sound, but nothing prepared me for the sheer size and bulk of the Wharton.

After we stowed our gear in our three-tier bunks, we brought our little USO bags up to the deck. The ship pulled away from the dock, people on shore waving to us, a mixture of hope and pride on their faces. I looked in my bag—a small tube of toothpaste and a toothbrush, a pen, a small pad of paper, cigarette lighter, cigarettes, razor, and a Baby Ruth. Since I didn't smoke, I traded my cigarettes for two more Baby Ruths, but I kept the lighter.

The first day aboard ship, as we sailed under the Golden Gate Bridge and into the Pacific Ocean, was the most miserable I ever spent at sea. The problem was, we didn't have any cargo—and without cargo for ballast, the Wharton bounced around like a cork in a swimming pool. Within an hour of leaving port, most of us were leaning over the rail or retching our Baby Ruths into our helmets. Following that ordeal, we were tasked to help keep our troop transport vessel ship-shape. My detail of three sailors painted the deck—a dull gray lead-based paint. The fumes alone caused us to reel again—but we stayed at it.

By the time we reached Seattle, most of us were five pounds lighter. I was hoping to get to see some of the city, but no liberty for anyone—besides it rained all the time. Around-the-clock, cargo and personnel were constantly being loaded onto the Wharton. So, we huddled in the galley and listened to the news for most of those three days, some conjecturing that the war would be over before we left port. Others guessed that we carried a secret payload or weapon that would end the war.

The USO showed up again, bundled up, standing in a slow mist, and handed more little bags to the 2,118 troops who boarded ship. Everything in the bag was the same except the candy bar—this time a Butterfinger. I traded my cigarettes and new lighter for three candy bars.

On Saturday, April 14, 1945, we steamed out of Seattle and into the Pacific. The wide blue horizon before us was endless, filled with uncertainty and hope. Our ship moved so slow, it felt like the Pacific was coming toward us, not us going toward it.

I looked around at my shipmates, all of us crowded by the rail—each holding their hats down into a steady wind and mist, faces grim—and I wondered which of us would never make it back.

8

When we stowed our gear next to our three-tiered bunks, mine always the middle bunk, we hooked our helmets to the bed above us. That way we'd be able to grab them in a moment's notice—if the USS Wharton was attacked, or if we had to throw-up again.

I quickly discovered the inequality between officers and enlisted men after we set sail from Seattle, and it wasn't just the steak and chicken cordon bleu they got to eat. We were told repeatedly in San Francisco and Seattle that we were not allowed to bring along cameras, no exceptions. The rationale was that if the enemy were to capture us, they would be able to learn where we had been and possibly decipher our movements and strategies from the pictures. A few times when I walked around on the Wharton, I spotted officers posing for photos, almost like they were on a cruise.

Everyone aboard ship, who was not a Marine or soldier being transported, was given duty. Eight hours on, eight hours off. You didn't get to choose what you wanted to do, or trade with someone else—we were assigned. Me? Along with five other sailors, we were tasked to climb down into the ship's massive storage hold and bring crates of food up to the galley. And to think, I initially asked to be in Cook and Baker School. How ironic.

With over 2,000 Marines and soldiers on board, some 30 Army nurses, and over 500 crew, food was needed around the clock in the chow hall. For me, that meant continually stooping down and winding my way up and down small, steep ladders and narrow gangways to get back and forth from the cargo hold to the galley. Initially, my 6'2" frame took a beating, my head banging into the openings between compartments, my skinny elbows on the sides. Within minutes of starting a shift, our light blue dungarees were soaked clear through with sweat. One good thing about that duty though—we were first in line for chow.

The USS Wharton was headed to Hawaii, a trip that would take two weeks. That's where we'd stop for a day to pick up more supplies and make small personnel changes. I didn't know it at the time, but I would be a total of five weeks on the Wharton and my final destination would be Okinawa—the island where more American and Japanese lives were lost than in any other battle during the war.

* * *

I got liberty in Honolulu and made the most of it, heading into Waikiki with some buddies. The first thing that struck me were all the bars, tattoo parlors, more bars, and more tattoo parlors—and gals in bright silk dresses everywhere. That night,

I spotted a sailor in front of a tattoo parlor, leaning on a chair, crying. He held a bottle of whiskey in one hand that he'd nip on, while a tattoo artist worked on his back. I looked over his shoulder and shuddered. A massive eagle covered his entire back, its talons dripping blood—real blood, not the tattoo kind. The Hawaiian culture fascinated me. I'd never seen so many dark-skinned natives, and such friendly people. The music, tiki torches, and exotic drinks were a hoot, too. We drank just enough not to come back to ship so drunk that we'd be put on report.

Honolulu was the last port where I would receive mail for a long time. Even though the three letters from Mother were weeks old, her gossip of our neighborhood, what my older brother Andy was doing in D.C., my younger brother and sister, the weather—it all came on me like a familiar warm blanket. Sometimes there'd be a "care" package waiting for me—some underwear, cookies, a book, toothbrush, a deck of cards. At this mail call, Mother sent me a jigsaw puzzle, custom made from a picture of our house. With every piece I joined together, I felt closer to my family, yet farther away from home.

Since we weren't allowed to write about where we were going, even if it was only rumors, I pretty much told her things were okay. I was healthy, and I missed her and the family, more than she knew. I did share some of what I learned during my medical training. Mother began to refer to me as her *little doctor*, and that always made me smile.

Our entertainment aboard the Wharton included cards and movies, and I didn't play cards. I saw *Anchors Aweigh* four times during our trip. It was ironic being on a troop transport ship headed into harms' way while Gene Kelly and Frank Sinatra sang and danced their version of what it was like to be in the Navy. When they crooned *We Hate to Leave*, I felt every word of it.

* * *

Eniwetok Atoll

The next day, we departed Hawaii for Eniwetok, a small atoll, part of the Marshall Islands, where we were to pick up further supplies. Being in the South Pacific, the heat and humidity was intense—so much so, that we were allowed to sleep on deck at night, the breeze providing somewhat of a cure for the stuffy, cramped bunks below.

Late one sleepless, moonless night, I made the mistake of taking out my lighter and flicking it. An officer ran toward me screaming, "What the hell are you doing, sailor?"

"Nothing, Sir."

"Put that away or deep six it, sailor." He planted his hands on his hips and squinted out at the dark horizon. "Just one flicker of light—sometimes that's all it takes for the Japs to spot a ship in the middle of the Pacific. Got it?"

"Aye, aye, Sir."

On the way to Eniwetok, I contracted something called cat fever—basically, a high temperature of unknown origin that was diagnosed as catarrhal fever. I was offended when the doctor questioned whether I visited whore houses, so prevalent in Honolulu, and caught some kind of disease. Whether he believed my denials or not, I got a full treatment of Penicillin that took hold in a couple of days. Today, doctors would probably say I had a bad cold and tell me to take some Tylenol, drink lots of fluids, and get plenty of rest.

Any sailor who cross the International Dateline for the first time was given a memento, mine issued to me on April 29, 1945.

Order of the Golden Dragon

Know all men that:

Hillhouse, Frederick S U.S.N.R. While on board the U.S.S. WHARTON having crossed the 180th Meridian at Lat. 13° N , is by virtue of having thus entered our **August Domain**, herewith and forever enlisted as a member of our order and shall be duly instructed in all the **Ancient Mysteries of the East** by all DRAGONS that he shall meet.

29 April 1945
(Date)

Supreme Golden Dragon

After Eniwetok, we were off to Ulithi, another atoll, but in the Caroline Islands, our final staging area before heading to Okinawa, the last stop for the US armed forces before the Japanese mainland. At Ulithi we made final adjustments to the crew and supplies. You could feel the tension build as each minute passed bringing us closer to our destination, and the rumors increased too. We heard that the Japs had a secret weapon they were going to use on us on Okinawa, that General MacArthur was coming aboard our ship, and many, many more.

On May 12, 1945, we left Ulithi and headed toward Okinawa. Sailors, called spotters, were spaced around the rail of the ship from stem to stern, holding large binoculars to their eyes. Their job was to look for any sign of submarines and also for Kamikaze suicide Japanese pilots who would take full payloads of bombs and gasoline and dive them directly into Navy ships. Already 38 US ships were lost to Kamikazes at Okinawa.

*   *   *

We received good news that in early April, the Yamato, the largest Japanese battleship in the world, heading from Japan to Okinawa to join in the fight against American forces, was destroyed. A collection of US submarines and 380 Navy aircraft sunk it in a single afternoon. With no fighters or destroyer escorts for its protection, the Yamato didn't stand a chance. In moments like that, when we heard of a huge victory, our spirits lifted—briefly. Then general quarters would sound, we'd all rush to our pre-assigned stations, strap on our helmets, and wait for our destruction—but not once were we attacked. Aside from periodic drills by our gunners, during the entire voyage from Seattle to Okinawa, we never fired our machine guns at an enemy.

On Saturday, May 19, 1945, the USS Wharton anchored off the east coast of Okinawa, near the destroyed town of Tokeshi, located just below the midpoint of the island. LCMs (Landing Craft Mechanized, we called them Mikes) shuttled out to us from shore to bring our 2,118 troops and supplies to the island, a task that would take a full week. Six times we went to general quarters and released huge smoke screens to disallow Jap suicide pilots from finding our ship to sink it.

LCMs (Mikes)

Weighed down with heavy packs, hand over hand we climbed down thick rope ladders thrown over the side of the Wharton and into the Mikes. It was during those moments I was most afraid—having come all this way, about to go ashore, only to not complete our mission.

That first afternoon when we landed on Okinawa, everyone in our unit took the small, collapsible shovels attached to our packs and dug ourselves foxholes on the beach, some of us running into trash left over from the previous soldiers who dug themselves in. We dined on cold rations, nothing to write home about, and were instructed to adhere to complete lights-out so as not to give Jap pilots easy targets to bomb or strafe at night.

Just before the sun set over the endless Pacific, I settled into my shallow hole in the sand, my helmet securely fastened under my chin, my carbine clutched in my hands. There's a smell to warm damp sand—almost like that cool patch of dirt under the front porch of your home on a hot summer day. I poked my head up and took in my surroundings—dotted all around me were hundreds of other sailors just like me, thousands of miles from home, on an island we never heard of before, hiding in holes.

If we survived that night, and the other nights to come, our job was to set up a military government hospital to aid the local civilians. But first we had to make it through the night. An air raid siren wailed to life, smoke bombs got released, and anti-aircraft rounds screamed into the night sky. I tried to shrink my 6'2" frame further into the bottom of my foxhole—and wondered which would find me first—sleep or death.

9

I woke up to the sound of propellers churning through water and wheels spinning in loose sand. I peeked over the edge of my foxhole to find more Mikes headed out to the Wharton and more coming back filled with men and supplies. Large dark green Army trucks moved slowly in an endless line along the beach, their gaping empty holds waiting to be filled.

I caught the eyes of some sailors a few foxholes away and gave a feeble "good morning" wave. A bullhorn down the beach squawked, "Gather your gear. We're moving out."

Like prairie dogs, heads popped up from all the foxholes and looked around. We hoisted our packs, grabbed our rifles, and moved toward the man with the bullhorn.

My stomach grumbled, and the sailor next to me, a skinny, curly-haired redhead noticed. He patted his belly and said, "Me too."

A makeshift chow line was set up a few hundred yards inland from the beach. That's where we were handed our nutritious, yet bland K-rations, and bottled water. By the time we finished eating what could barely be called food at seven o'clock, we were already sweating from the heat and humidity.

In the far distance, low rumbles, almost like thunder, drifted through the lush tropical trees. I looked up, not a cloud in the sky. Someone nearby said, "They're shelling mountain caves—that's where most of the Japs are hiding."

As I took that in, Chief Warrant Officer Briggs blared through his bullhorn for us to follow him as our Lieutenant Commander had something to say. All 200 of us gathered to hear the latest—rumors, as always, rippling through the ranks about what was coming. The usual, *the war was over, we've being reassigned,* you know.

"It's going to take some time, possibly a few days, for us to receive all our equipment and set up our hospital. We already know of hundreds of local natives who are in desperate need of medical care. Tonight's quarters will be off the beach and in caves, a bit of a hike from here. Chief Warrant Officer Briggs will give you your assignments."

We were led on a three-mile hike, climbing ever higher, until we reached a large grouping of caves. Army trucks followed us up the hill. From the back of the trucks, we each grabbed a cot and lugged our duffle bags, rifles, and packs into the caves. Against one wall of dirt, we wedged the cots. That left just enough room for us to shuffle by. We stuffed our bags underneath the cots, tossed our packs on top, and headed outside with our rifles.

After a boring day of cold rations and loose patrol, in case any stray enemy was about, we settled into another near-sleepless night. No one wanted to say it, but as small bits of dirt crumbled down on us while we tossed and turned, the horror of our cave collapsing and burying us alive was not far from our thoughts.

The next morning, we were awakened by the groan of more Army trucks laboring up the hill. We hit the cold K-ration chow line where 'word' got passed around that we were moving out of Tokeshi and headed north to Kushi on the western side of the island to set up our hospital. We boarded transport trucks, crammed in shoulder-to-shoulder, our heavy packs on our backs, rifles held in our hands, and our duffle bags wedged between our knees.

After a bouncing three-hour drive over rough dirt roads, most one-lane mountain paths, we got out to stretch our legs, relieve ourselves, and grab more rations. Then it was back in the trucks. Four hours later we arrived in Kushi. I'd never been so glad to get out of a vehicle in my life, my legs cramped and my behind sore from a day of bouncing on a hard wooden bench—and my face covered in dust and soot from the open back of the truck.

Since our sleep quarters were not yet ready, we were led to a deserted schoolhouse where we bunked down for the night. We opened all the windows and prayed for some kind of breeze, anything to help cool down the night. When distant machine gun fire interrupted our sleep, we dove under our cots and stayed put until it ceased.

The next morning, we searched the local caves for people, weapons and such. In one we found crates full of horseshoes, and a dozen large boxes full of Japanese condoms. I wondered what kind of party they planned to have. Ha!

With buddy Al Stahnke at a ruined cemetery on Okinawa

The next morning, we were organized into groups to build a perimeter fence. For the next three days, we slogged through swamp-like grass, dug holes, filled them with poles and cement, and strung security lines and barbed wire. At the end of each day, we were exhausted, our clothes and bodies soaked in a kind of purple stain from the muck. My thoughts drifted back to my

65

first job at Savage Arms Munitions, only three years ago, and my grease-stained hands and clothes. I couldn't help but wonder if I made the rifle I now kept nearby.

The brief, cold, make-shift showers were welcome relief from both the heat and purple stain. Basically, a bucket of water to get you wet, soap up, and another bucket to rinse you off. The hardest part was getting rid of the smell—a mix between rotten eggs and spoiled milk, a place I never wish to visit again.

* * *

The supplies and equipment to build our housing and large hospital tents finally arrived, and within three days we were set up. Generators hummed day and night, providing electricity for lights and fans. The Army sent out translators to contact the local natives, civilians who were hiding in caves, trying to stay out of the fighting.

The first to arrive was a mother with a sick child, followed by an elderly man with a nasty skin rash. After word got out that America built a hospital to help them, people streamed in. Some of the younger native women already trained to be nurses, joined us to care for their own people and provide limited translation capabilities.

Late Friday afternoon, June 22, 1945, almost exactly one month after the USS Wharton dropped us off on an Okinawa beach, our P.A. system crackled to life with an energetic voice announcing that the Japs surrendered Okinawa. Bill Abbott, another pharmacist mate who trained with me back in San

Bruno, California, celebrated with me the best we knew how, dancing with nurses as speakers around our camp blared swing music from the Andrew Sisters and Ella Fitzgerald.

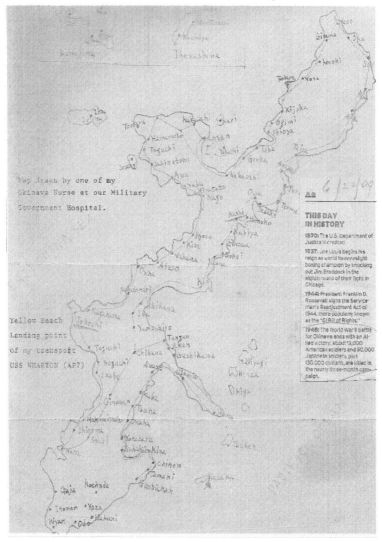

A handmade map of Okinawa one of the native nurses gave me, plus a news clipping

The ballroom dance moves I learned from the Steele sisters when I was 14, came back to me. Sliding around in my boots on a dirt floor 10,000 miles from home—that was as far away as I could get from the polished wood parlor where I was taught the 'perfect' frame back in Utica.

The toll from the fighting on Okinawa was staggering: Just over 14,000 allied troops died; 110,000 Japanese killed; and, half of the 300,000-native population died or committed suicide during the 82-day battle.

* * *

The following day, supplies for two Quonset huts showed up along with a group of Seabees. Within a week, these structures took shape—one building to be used for an office and the officers' quarters, the other as a surgery center. That would have opened sooner, but somewhere along the supply line, someone hijacked our ice machine, needed for so many treatments. Secretly, I hoped to see those ice cubes clinking in a high ball, awaiting a mixed drink.

The most unusual native I treated was an old man named Po. He had a shrapnel wound. A shard of metal had pierced the upper part of his calf and exited at his heal. Initially, I thought he packed his wound with rice, maybe some kind of native treatment. But on closer inspection, the rice was moving—it was maggots. Initially repulsed, I consulted a doctor and he recommended I flush out the wound with alcohol. It took four small cans to rinse out all the fly larvae. I dressed Po's wound and treated it every day for three weeks until he was able to leave.

He bowed several times, shook my hand, and said something in his language that I didn't know, but fully understood, then he hobbled away on a cane.

* * *

In early September, we got the news that on Monday, August 6 at 8:15 am, the US parachuted a 9,000-pound atomic bomb down to 2,000 feet above Hiroshima and detonated it. In a flash, five square miles were destroyed and 40,000 people incinerated. I couldn't imagine a weapon like that, with so many people killed in an instant. It overwhelmed me. Three days later, on Thursday, August 9th at 11:02 am, the same fate befell the city of Nagasaki.

Hiroshima after the A-bomb

The Japanese officially surrendered on Sunday, September 2, 1945. The news descended on our encampment like a fresh wave, sweeping away the horrors of the past four years, breathing hope into all our hearts.

* * *

We didn't get any liberty on Okinawa, mainly because there was no town to go to, no bars to frequent, and no gals to take dancing. Yet on Wednesday, September 26, we all boarded Army transport trucks and were hauled a few hours away to the Naval Supply Depot at Tengan. I was too far from the stage to appreciate the performances of the Charlie Ruggles USO Show, but I did remember Emma Lou Welch singing with him, Virginia Caroll dancing, and Arthur Zepp on the piano accompanied by an orchestra.

Two weeks later, on the morning of Tuesday, October 9, Typhoon Louise hit the island. We thought we were prepared, but as the hours passed, both the rain and winds steadily increased, battering everything in its path. The lights flickered and went out, our P.A. system died—nothing but howling, unabated wind shrieking at us. We heard canvas being torn and the flapping of loose wet tents nearby, and even muffled yells from men caught unawares.

I went to a corner of our tent and wedged myself into the canvas to try to hold it down. Along with other sailors, we did our best to keep back the unrelenting storm. We couldn't. First, a tear in one corner, then another in our roof. Not long after, the driving rain found its way under our tent skirts and flooded our dwelling. We heard later that the winds reached far above 100 miles per hour, and it made sense when the sides and roof of our tent were torn from its moorings, exposing us to the full force of the typhoon at sunset. As we fumbled about trying to figure out our next move, I felt a mixture of fear and awe as I watched palm trees get uprooted and even spotted a truck on its side.

We were completely drenched by the time we dragged what we could into caves above us to get out of the howling wind and rain. In the early morning light, we came out and surveyed the damage. Typhoon Louise had done its job, squashing our tents, even leveling the Quonset huts. It was if a massive army of nature trampled everything in its path.

It took us two days to get anything dry and another week to get some semblance of order back in the hospital. Al Stahnke built us a new hut while I provided moral support. I didn't know it at the time, but three weeks later, I'd leave Okinawa and begin my long trek home—to Mother's stuffed pork chops, and my local bar where I could toss back a few with my friends, and forget all about typhoons and maggots.

10

Points. That's what I finally tallied enough of to begin my long trek home. Days in, combat, theaters of war, rank—they all added up. By the time I would get discharged months later, I would total up 1,225 days in the Navy.

My first orders took me on a transport plane to the Atsugi Honshu Airfield in Japan. I was to wait there until 89 other sailors joined me to take the LST (Landing Ship Tank) 1071 back to the US of A. We stayed in the abandoned Japanese barracks at the airfield. Everything about the place was small, especially for my 6'2" frame. I stooped to use the showers, squatted way down to sit on a john, ducked under doorways, and my feet dangled out the end of my bunk.

We got leave a few times and hitched military rides into the nearby town of Yokosuka. It was all about sightseeing for me and my friends, with orders of no drinking allowed, not even the saké. Here we were, miles from home, three months after *the bomb* dropped, strolling the streets of a Japanese city, something I never expected to happen in my life. We were told to be on the lookout for dissidents and possible trouble, but shore patrol was everywhere.

First impressions? The Japanese people, mostly women and old men, were small and polite, constantly lowering their heads and bowing. The women wore bright-colored kimonos and wooden shoes, walking in short choppy steps. Some even looked like porcelain dolls. I was so taken with their get-ups that one of the native nurses gave me two silk kimonos and two pairs of wooden shoes.

I'm on the top left with a moustache!

My last Thanksgiving in the Navy was at the airfield. Walking into the mess hall, it was the smell that hit me first— home. I don't know how the cooks did it, but we had carved turkey, stuffing, mashed potatoes, gravy, green beans, ambrosia, cranberries, and biscuits. Lots of biscuits. I even grabbed a few and stuffed them in my jacket to munch on later.

Talk around the table was all about going home. I posed a question. "What do you miss most? Or a better question is, what will you do first?"

It got quiet for a few moments as everyone reached deep to find that empty space they'd shoved aside during the past three years. Some of the answers surprised me.

"If it's still running, or my little brother didn't wreck it, I'd jump in my '38 Buick Coupe and drive until I run outta gas," Greeley said, while he twisted his arms in front of him like he was steering his car.

"Hold my girl. Then propose to her," Roberts grinned.

"Sit down for a meal with my family. And I don't care what we're eating." Gallagher stuffed his mouth full of turkey and cranberries, smiling, hit teeth stained with the mess.

"Reverend Baxter. I'd go talk to him," Williams said, his eyes downcast.

The guys got all quiet after that. We knew some of us saw things we might never get over or out of our minds. We didn't get around to me, but my answer would have been simple—a plate of Mother's stuffed pork chops with my family and catching a Broadway musical.

* * *

We stayed at the airfield through Christmas where they fed us another big meal, pretty much matching what we had for Thanksgiving, but throwing in baked ham with mint jelly. There was a relaxed tension to everything because we were still so far from home. We also heard stories about Japs who hadn't heard the war was over and were still killing US troops.

A package from home arrived. Mother included the usual clean underwear and socks and a letter with all the goings-on from their new home in Buffalo. She also tossed in some cookies and candy she knew I'd like. That care package tugged on me more than the others, a hard reminder of how far away from home I was—and how long it would take to get back there.

The most fun we had over the holidays was watching the movie *The Outlaw* three times. That was the Howard Hughes film starring Jane Russell with her infamous low-cut peasant blouse, laying back in a mound of hay, inviting Billy the Kid to join her. You should have heard the hoots and hollers from the guys, another reminder of my home.

I was transferred to relieve a First Class Pharmacist Mate on a LST. He was heading home like me on points. Before he left he received extra supplies from other ships that were being decommissioned.

After I took over the 5x8 sick bay, I went over the inventory of the narcotics in the supply locker. I had way too many than I was supposed to have according to the log. So I gathered the extra pills, and without telling anyone, tossed them overboard when we got out to sea. I think some fish had a good time.

On December 27, we departed Japan and headed for Guam on the USS Ouachita County (LST 1071), a 328-foot-long landing ship. As usual for me, the first day-and-a-half out of port, I was seasick, saltine crackers and water my medicine. The good news was that my only duty on ship was to run our little sickbay, to handle most everything from a headache to athlete's foot—and I got to set my hours. Any serious disease or ailment, sailors would be transferred to a hospital. No one wanted that, because they all wanted to get home. So, no one got sick.

Captain Gilliam was a school teacher in real life, and we all guessed his students hated him. He barked out orders he often countermanded. He forced the cooks to put cheese in everything, and I mean everything. A small group of sailors asked me to intervene, but I got nowhere with the captain.

The day before we arrived in Guam, the captain found an axe embedded in his stateroom door. That really set him off. No one came forward with an admission of guilt, even though the captain threatened the crew with severe punishment. After we docked, he was transferred to a transport plane that took him home, also because he had high points making him eligible for returning home. I think that was best. We got a new captain.

For New Years' Eve in Guam, we all went ashore for a beer party and swimming. No gals, just the guys blowing off steam and celebrating our freedom from cheese oppression. When we left Guam for Hawaii just two days into the new year, the same seasickness hit me for 36 hours. We traveled alongside another LST which had some engine trouble, so we moved slowly with it always in sight.

Like all captains, ours kept alcohol supplies in his stateroom for obvious reasons—so that the crew wouldn't indulge. I had a small amount to be used in sickbay.

Motor Machinist Mate Tommy O'Reilly, a short redheaded Irishman with more freckles than stars, came to me. I already heard of some of his shenanigans with booze. "Fred, can ya help me here?"

"Are you asking what I think you are, O'Reilly?"

"Ever had torpedo juice? It's a kick in the head."

"Yeah, I read about it, and got a Navy directive somewhere in…" I pulled open a drawer and shuffled through some papers. Really, I was stalling for time. Out of the corner of my eye, I could see O'Reilly was antsy, doing almost an Irish jig in anticipation. "You know, it's 190-proof pure grain alcohol, and they put some nasty additives in it."

"I'm just trying to get a little party going."

"Well, that party might make you go blind or worse," I said with my best authoritative hands-on-hips stance.

"And?"

"Jiminy Cricket, O'Reilly. People have died from this. How 'bout I make you some bilge juice—yeast, water, and sugar. I could have a batch ready in a week or so."

O'Reilly winced at the thought. "Doc, you know, you can filter the torpedo juice through a loaf of bread or distill it down," his eyes pleaded.

"If I did, it'd be for sippin', nothing else."

He shook my hand and shot out the door before I could change my mind. While I figured out how to get my hands on some torpedo juice, O'Reilly was up to his antics. He got some booze from another ship, went to the bow with a few other guys and celebrated their journey home. None of them showed up in sickbay, so I figured I'd try my hand at bartending. I went to the galley, got some pineapple juice and powdered drink mix, both lemon and orange.

I told the captain I needed more denatured alcohol to handle some of the guys' cuts and scrapes. He handed me a one-gallon jug. "Is this good enough to get you started, Hillhouse?"

You bet.

"Aye, aye, Captain."

Once I perfected the concoction, which I sampled numerous times, I invited O'Reilly, who'd become a close friend, to join me for *cocktail hour.*

When sickbay wasn't open, I either slept in my bunk, read a book, hung out with the chefs in the galley, or took in the deck. Up there, it was nothing but endless blue horizons, and fresh breezes so strong, I had to stow my hat or lose it.

During our trip to Hawaii, I had one patient in sickbay who really needed help. Albert Swanson came in limping real bad. I thought it might be a sprained ankle. That was, until he pulled off his shoes and socks. He had by far the worst case of athlete's foot I ever saw, even worse than in textbook pictures. In the old days, it was called ringworm of the foot. The technical term was *tinea pedis*. Whatever it was, thick chunks of skin peeled off between his toes and even the bottoms of his feet, exposing raw, bleeding flesh.

"Doc, what can you do for me?"

"How long you had this, Swanson?" I asked, spreading his toes apart with a tongue depressor.

"For a couple months now."

"And, you're just now seeing someone?"

"Yup."

I looked him in the eyes. "I've got to tell you, Swanson, this might be so bad, we'll have you transferred to a hospital."

He shook his head, grabbed his socks and started to put them on.

"Hold on now," I continued. "Let's see what I can do first."

We were three weeks away from Hawaii, and with no ports along the way, there was no means to get him to a hospital anyway. I started his treatment with some phenol and camphor on his feet, and made him some gauze socks. "I'm writing you an order for new shoes. In fact, we'll change them every other day. And when you get your feet wet, and I mean wet at all, you come see me. Got it?"

"Sure, doc."

By the time we got to Hawaii, Swanson's feet almost looked normal. The only other injury we had was *after* we anchored in Hawaii. I was out on shore leave when a sailor tumbled down the gangway, ending up in a heap at the bottom.

He was taken to the hospital with a broken ankle and I never saw him again.

Two days later, we shoved off for San Diego. The voyage took less than a week, and without incident, arriving on February 5, 1946, early in the afternoon. I didn't think about how I'd feel stepping ashore, onto American soil again. It stirred a longing for everything I missed for the past 1,200 days.

Twenty-five more to go.

Almost home.

11

Beer. In so many ways, coming back to the USA was all about beer. Our first day of liberty, a group of us, dressed in our Navy whites with all our ribbons, took a water taxi from Coronado over to San Diego. We headed downtown to the Horton Park Fountain. A handful of bums, you'd call them homeless today, washed their faces in the fountain and begged for change, but we declined. Bars were sandwiched side-to-side on surrounding streets with a few tattoo parlors and girlie shows breaking up the monotony.

Downtown San Diego's Horton Plaza 1946

We started at a bar in the northeast corner and made our way from one to another, drinking nothing but beer. It didn't take long before everyone in every bar knew we'd just come back from Okinawa.

"Let me buy you guys a round," we heard everywhere we went. I lost count of how many I had to drink by ten o'clock. We got so drunk, five of us got a room at the US Grant Hotel. I woke up the next morning, greeted by a dull headache, but also the sweet sounds of traffic below our fourth-floor room.

Beer. That's how I spent the next four days. On February 10, 1946, we took our LST-1071 toward Northern California where we anchored right across from San Quentin State Penitentiary at the north end of the San Francisco Bay. We went ashore the first day of liberty and found a fresh set of bars and more beer. Me and two buddies lost track of time and missed the last boat back to our ship, so we ended up spending the night in the San Quentin Guard House.

I don't remember more than a little history the caretaker told us about the prison. "San Quentin is the oldest state penitentiary in California, founded sometime in the mid-1800s. Some of the famous criminals who were housed here include Black Bart, whose real name was Charles Bolles—he robbed Wells Fargo gold shipments in the late 1800s. Then there was famous forger Joseph Cosey who was arrested after selling fake Abraham Lincoln letters."

After that, I got too tired to listen anymore and fell asleep on one of the cots he set up for us, my feet dangling over the edge.

I'm second from the left with my moustache and drinking buddies

After a few days of liberty in San Francisco bars, we were shuttled over to Treasure Island, smack dab between San Francisco and Oakland in the middle of the bay. I was surprised to discover it was an artificial/manmade island built ten years before and used for the 1939 Golden Gate Exposition. There I received orders to transfer me to Sampson Air Force Base in upstate NY for my discharge from the Navy. I was finally going home.

PACFLEET 111

UNITED STATES NAVY

U. S. S. LST 1071

NAME HILLHOUSE, Frederick S.

RANK
RATE PhM2/c

FILE OR
SERVICE NO. 600-85-71

IS HEREBY AUTHORIZED TO WEAR THE RIBBONS INDICATED ON THE REVERSE SIDE. UNAUTHORIZED WEARING OF DEC-ORATIONS IS A VIOLATION OF UNIFORM REGULATIONS AND WILL RESULT IN APPROPRIATE DISCIPLINARY ACTION.

18 Jan., 1946

Date   Title:

I crossed America by train most of the way, bus the last legs—all the way from Oakland, California to Romulus, New York. The trip was nothing but a blur of glasses of beer in the dining car mixed with the constant clack of metal wheels rolling over the seams of nearly 3,000 miles of metal tracks. Having achieved the rank of Pharmacist Mate 2/C, following hundreds of hours of study, treating patients with impaction to maggot-infested wounds to athlete's foot, traveling half way around the world—I received my honorable discharge on February 12, 1946. When Master Chief Gallo smashed his blue stamp on my discharge form and handed it to me, it was over—my 1,225 days in the US Navy.

With travel vouchers in hand, I went from bus to train and arrived in Buffalo half a day later. Jerry, another sailor, came along for the ride. While I was away, my parents moved from Utica to Buffalo, Dad getting another promotion from the A&P. They had a small 'Welcome Home' party waiting for me that night, but I wasn't ready to go home just yet.

Instead, Jerry and I lugged our duffle bags to Club Romney over on Broadway and Rommel Streets. We shared our Navy stories with each other until we were the only ones there at closing, the bartender calling us cabs. Even that ride was free. We pulled up in front of my parents' new home, the front door light on and an upstairs bedroom lit. A small banner was strung between the two square pillars on the porch, my name in gold and red letters. I felt bad about missing all their plans and the hoopla, but I didn't miss having to explain my three-and-a-half years away over and over to a handful of neighbors.

"How'd you sleep, Frederick?" Mother asked when I stumbled into the kitchen the next morning around noon.

"Fine. Just fine." I rubbed my scruffy face trying to get it fully awake.

She opened the Fridgidaire and pulled out eggs and milk. "French toast, just the way you like it?"

I yawned and stretched my arms above my head, then looked around. "Sure. Hey, where's Daddy and my brother and sister?"

"You know, you missed a wonderful party last night."

I watched, almost like it was my first time, as she cracked two eggs into a glass mixing bowl, added a splash of milk, a few shakes of salt, tossed in a teaspoon of sugar, and some vanilla, sprinkled in cinnamon, and brought out the hand mixer. When she began to crank it, I noticed how old her hands had become, brown spots dotting her white Belgian skin—or maybe they were always that way.

"Yeah, sorry about that," I said.

She began to hum, something I forgot she did when she cooked. The softness of her voice teased out happy childhood memories—mostly of meals together or coming into our warm home from playing in the snow. As she placed two slices of egg-soaked bread into the hot cast-iron skillet, I stood up, went to her, and gave her a hug. She froze, unaccustomed to displays of affection from her children—then eased into me. Prince Matchabelli perfume and scalding butter filled my nose.

Home.

* * *

During the ensuing weeks, I discovered all the bars in Buffalo while I tried to figure out what to do next. I saved nearly $1,000, nowhere to spend it really when I was in the Navy. I knew what I did not want to do, work in an ammunitions company, or clean wounds. Bartending sounded like an ideal vocation for me, but I knew my parents wouldn't approve. So, my semi-search for a career languished.

One evening, after listening to *The Adventures of Ellery Queen* on the radio in the den with Dad, I found myself alone with him, a rarity. He wore his maroon smoking jacket, had a highball next to him, and was forever messing with his pipe, trying to get the tobacco tamped down just right so it would stay lit.

"How'd you like the show, Daddy?"

"It was a good one, Frederick. I always enjoy how you can never quite figure out who's the guilty one, but Ellery can."

"Yeah." A question that'd been gnawing at me for the past few years, gurgled up into my throat. At nearly twenty-five years old, it surprised me. "Do you think you could call me Fred now, and not Frederick?"

He scraped the dottle from his pipe into the ashtray and tapped out the last bits. He looked at me with a knowing smile. "I will, but only if you stop calling me daddy, and call me dad instead."

And just like that, I was all grown up.

12

A month passed and I still didn't have a clue what to do next. I spoke with my Aunt Ruth, who lived in Connecticut, the aunt who used to live in New York City and took me to Broadway shows. She put the idea in my head.

"Why not move down to the City, Frederick?"

I stared at the receiver. I'd been to the Big Apple plenty of times for plays and musicals. I also remembered that my parents honeymooned at the Breslin Hotel over on West 29th near 5th Avenue. That's how their lives started. Maybe mine could start in New York City as well. "Great idea, Aunt Ruth."

I really knew nothing about Buffalo. It was my parents' home, not mine. And there was something gnawing at me—3½ years in the Navy with only a few days of liberty here or there. I needed a vacation, actually an extended vacation. A week later, I took the train from Buffalo to the City and found my way to the Breslin Hotel. My room was nothing to speak of. I couldn't imagine my parents honeymooning there almost thirty years before and any romance that might have occurred.

Even though it was chilly, I wanted to take in as much of the City as possible, so I walked the ten blocks to Times Square. I didn't know it at the time, but this would become my stomping grounds for the next two years. Every bar in the area had its own clientele, décor, shows, some with cover charges. I tried them all and, within a week, settled on the Metropole as my favorite, with its huge rectangular bar and a large stage behind it for all the dancers and singers. A Miller draft beer in a frosted glass only cost 50 cents.

After a week in the City, I contacted William Hillhouse, a younger redheaded cousin who lived in Rutherford, New Jersey. "Bill, I'm in the City and looking for job. Any ideas?"

"I'll put out the word, Fred."

We did more catching up on the phone, then I headed back to the Metropole. A few days later, Bill called back with a suggestion from a friend who worked at Chase National Bank near the New York Stock Exchange. He told me to apply for a job and I'd get in. It was that easy.

I took a room in a boarding house over on Columbus Avenue near 81st Street for five bucks a week. It was clean. Bathroom down the hall. Noisy neighbors upstairs with their loud radio and stomping around, a crying baby next door. Nothing I couldn't handle, especially when I compared it to a foxhole on an Okinawa beach with Jap bombs falling all around me.

None of that mattered. I was living in New York City.

Times Square 1946

The mail room. Actually, the mail desk. That's where I stood every morning, at Miss Marian Pulver's desk on the tenth floor of the Chase National Bank. Her small frame shook with a constant nervousness and her 60-something pinched face couldn't hide her delight at making me and my co-worker wait while she put on her glasses and slowly sorted through the mail.

"This one's for you, Fred," she said, handing me a large envelope with foreign stamps plastered all over the front.

Without looking up, she continued, "Joe, this is yours," she said to Joe Kistinger, my co-worker who handled domestic mail, and who would become a good friend.

Miss Pulver continued with the uncluttering of her desk until our arms were filled with dozens of envelopes. Mine held the financial hopes and dreams of businesses and wealthy individuals from around the world.

"Now, off you go, the both of you." She waved the back of her hand at us like she was shooing away flies.

Dressed in my crisp new dark suit and tie, I sat at my desk, opened the first envelope and dove in. By the time I finished reading the letter inside, I was filled with more questions than when I took medical training in the Navy. Instead of life or death decisions about war injuries and illnesses though, these were all financial decisions. Just as I was about to get up to see Miss Pulver, she showed up at my desk.

"Because most of these customers don't know English very well, it takes a little more time to comprehend what they want, Fred." She looked at me with understanding eyes, a surprise. "Why don't you show me what's got you stumped and we'll work through it together?"

* * *

At 11:30, a bell rang, and Joe came over to my desk. "Come on, Fred. Hurry."

I followed him down the crowded elevator to the ground floor, and out the front door of the bank. Two blocks away, we entered a building and took the elevator up to the tenth floor. It was the distinct aroma of beef stroganoff that hit me first. "What the…?"

"Time for lunch, Fred," Joe said.

We walked into a huge dining room, the kind you'd find in a nice restaurant—not a fancy one, but nice. Joe led me to a table with a window overlooking Wall Street Avenue, where I could see thousands of people pouring out of buildings, going for lunch. I followed his lead as he picked up the menu, a waitress appearing instantly.

"I'll have an ice tea and the veal parmigiana, and..." Joe turned to me.

"I'll do the same," I mumbled.

She took our menus and I watched her move on to an adjacent table to take their orders. I leaned toward Joe and whispered, "I didn't see any prices. How much—"

"Don't worry, Fred. It's free for bank employees. Salad and desert too. Oh, and if you don't like what's on the menu, they'll make you three sandwiches, usually roast beef."

Just as he said that, a server arrived with salads and desert for both of us.

That was the highlight of my first day of work at Chase National Bank in New York City.

* * *

Breakfast every morning was at Nedick's. It seemed like one of their kiosks was on every corner in the City, kind of like how Starbucks are now. For 15 cents, I'd get an orange juice, a glass of milk, and a donut—glazed being my favorite.

Sometimes after lunch, Joe and I would walk around Wall Street. If the weather was bad, we'd go into the balcony of the NYSE and watch men down on the floor until it was time to go back to work. Frantic voices yelled while men in suits waved their arms through the thick cigarette smoke—one of the best show we'd ever seen.

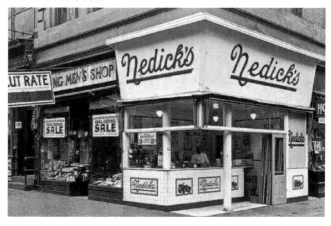

*   *   *

I quickly settled into a routine. Up at six every morning, shave and shower down the hall, aftershave, fresh shirt and tie, cuff links, tie clip, watch. I was never a "hat" guy, so I didn't worry about that, but Brill Cream and a fine-tooth comb kept my hair in place and looking sharp. I took the subway to the financial district, stopped by Nedick's, and was in the office by eight o'clock. Lunched with Joe, then usually stopped by the Metropole after work for a beer, only one beer, before heading home, especially if it was a week night.

My first paycheck was a stark surprise. $80 every two weeks—one dollar an hour, before taxes. With rent at five bucks a week, five cent subway fares, draft Millers at fifty cents, club/bar cover charges at twenty-five cents, ten cents to launder and starch my shirts, fifteen cents for breakfast—it disappeared fast, including my savings. Mother, in her all-knowing and caring way, sensed my demise. Every week, while I lived in the City, she sent me a little note and twenty dollars.

Thanks, Mom.

To make things stretch even further, I always kept a jar of Skippy peanut butter and saltine crackers on the window sill of my room, to snack on if my stomach growled.

* * *

I dressed like I had money. Suit and tie to work, two overcoats—a black Chesterfield with a velvet collar once owned by my older brother, and a Camel hair full-length. Weekends were slacks, a sports shirt, and leisure jacket. If you haven't figured it out by now, that's where the rest of my money went, to clothes. The remainder I spent on good times at the nightclubs and bars in the City, staying out both Friday and Saturday nights until the bars closed at four a.m.

A visit to the Bronx Zoo in 1946

Besides my favorite, the Metropole, I found my way around to other clubs. There was the Sawdust Trail Bar where almost anyone could take the stage and perform, and the twenty-five-cent cover charge kept the "riff-raff" out. I saw Jo Sullivan there—she ended up marrying Frank Loesser, a big Broadway producer. I caught Theresa Brewer's act there too. She was a little thing of a performer who ended up singing "Music, Music, Music," which became her signature song.

With Mary Mason and her friend

I also met Mary Mason, a talented singer in the Sawdust and we really hit it off. I loved her smooth singing style and look. After a few months of taking in her act and kind of dating, even meeting her family, she asked me to be her manager. For a ten percent fee, I would need to line up performances for her in clubs around The City. I thought about it real hard and realized it was just too risky for me to quit my job at the bank—and having her depend on me for her livelihood was too much. I declined, but we remained friends.

Everything about The Plaza Hotel & Bar was pure class, from the doorman's nod to the frosted glasses for my Millers. I enjoyed hanging out with Jack Dempsey at his bar/restaurant—he greeted everyone at the door. Great guy with huge fists and a bigger laugh. At the Commodore Hotel & Bar, I met Esmond Knight, a British actor who just finished filming *The River*, a movie that was made in India. What a wonderful guy—and so very British in everything he did, like the way he held out his perfectly manicured pinkie finger when he drank.

I used to frequent the Astor Hotel's bar, and my favorite place to meet friends was under the huge lobby clock with its resounding dong every hour. I met actor John Howard coming off the elevator with his wife, Kathryn Grayson, a beautiful singer, and she joined us in a brief conversation. They gave me their autographs, a highlight of the night for me.

I'd also drop into the Stork Club and pop into the 21 Bar occasionally. Then there was The Waldorf Astoria in the lower bar—very, very nice. And every once in a while, a friend of mine who worked at JP Morgan would join me in the Penthouse

Club at the top of a building on 59th Street overlooking Central Park. A thick steak with all the trimmings—tasty!

Oh, and one of my other favorite places was Sammy's Bowery Follies. I had to take the Third Avenue El to get there, but it was worth it. I became such a traveling regular, that the El cashier once invited me into his booth for a little talk while I waited to catch a ride. Sammy's was a beer joint with sawdust on the floor, a big, long polished mahogany bar, and bowls of peanuts where you could throw the shells on the floor. A well-lit stage, and a piano player highlighted a bevy of beauties singing Gay 90's musical classics. I'd never join in, instead buying drinks for the girls at the bar.

* * *

As I walked home from an evening out, I came upon a theatre on 7th Avenue that was having an opening night. I joined the crowd to watch the celebrities enter, the only ones I recognized were the Duke and Duchess of Windsor. They were royally dressed and much shorter than I imagined.

After the show began, I popped into a crowded bar next door. I excused myself and reached between two women to get a drink—and realized one was movie actress Nancy Carroll. Well, we struck up a conversation, her friend a fashion designer. Somewhere during our chat, she suggested that I meet her daughter, Patricia Kirkland, also an actress. I guess I looked the right age and was presentable.

Nancy Carroll

Ah, New York City. I breathed it in. I drank it in. I took it all in.

13

Instead of taking the subway home one night, I decided to walk through Central Park and began ambling down 5th Avenue. I spotted a tall, thin man ahead of me strolling in a dark Chesterfield coat, a Hamburg slanted on his head. Just by his walk, I could tell there was something special about him, an unusual gait. I caught up to him and we stopped to talk for a few minutes, then continued walking together.

He carried a Bible and told me how he just came from a reading at a radio station. It was actor John Carradine! I remembered him from Frankenstein and Dracula movies. What a voice, so deep and purposeful. When we approached 59th Street we said our goodbyes, he to The Plaza and me headed home—carrying the memories of his rich voice with me all the way home.

* * *

I didn't have enough money to go to all the plays and musicals which were such a passion of mine—but I had a front row seat to the greatest show on earth, the people and the nightlife of New York City. Speaking of the greatest show on earth, each year I attended Ringling Bros. Barnum & Bailey Circus. I got to know Felix Adler, the famous clown, and other entertainers, meeting them before and after their shows at local clubs. What impressed me most about the circus was Gargantua, the massive gorilla they kept in a cage. He reminded me of King Kong and Mighty Joe Young.

* * *

It took almost a year before I got promoted at the bank, and at the same time Miss Pulver was let go. I went on to the export letters of credit desk, Joe to import letters of credit. I know what you're going to ask, why kind of raise did I get? How about five cents an hour! Wahoo! That was two dollars more a week. I didn't know how Joe did it living in Yonkers, being married and all.

I held my first baby, theirs, and his pretty little wife Peggy told me, "You look so good with a baby, Fred. When do you think you'll start a family?"

I smiled and handed the baby to Joe. "Yours is good enough for me right now."

That tugged on me a little, but with the small amount of money I made, getting married or buying a home were out of the question. I did occasionally see Doris, a cute gal from Washington, D.C.—brunette, glasses, a great sense of humor. That worked out well for a while, even double-dating with some mutual friends.

She worked at US Steel and would get free tickets to Yankee games—in the president box, right behind the dugout. That's when I got to see my doppelganger Joe DiMaggio up close. She invited me to rent bikes and join her for a memorable Saturday ride across town to 125th Street and the Hudson River. There we took a ferry over to New Jersey and pedaled around Palisades Park, picnicking and enjoying a perfect summer day. I remember looking over at her and wondering if she could be *the one* for me. Those thoughts left quickly when I realized the meager amount of money I made was barely enough for me, let alone a wife.

We took the ferry back to Manhattan and ended a lovely day. She told me that her time in the City was over, unable to afford the cost of living there—and that she was moving back to her hometown of Utica. She gave me a look, her eyes wondering if I felt the same, that maybe I'd join her.

"Good luck, Doris. I hope you do well there."

I took over her furnished room on the East Side for $7.50 a week (and it even had a sink). Closer to work and closer to the Metropole.

I managed to see one play, standing room only for the opening night of *Liliom*, with incredible performances by Ingrid Bergman and Burgess Meredith. During intermission in the lobby, I met stars Gene Raymond (who was married to Jeanette MacDonald), Douglas Montgomery, and Christopher Morely— collecting their autographs on the playbill.

* * *

Making ends meet in New York City got to be a real challenge. Ray Bacon, a co-worker at Chase, told me over lunch one day about some of his "side" work. He donated blood for $20 a pint, but could only do that every six weeks. He also worked as a model for western serial magazines, dressing up as a cowboy for some of articles and covers. I thought about doing the same—with selling my blood and acting—but I didn't feel that desperate.

* * *

In the dead of winter, after a Saturday night of drinking, something about being alone in the big city came down on me hard. I looked up at the second-story window at the room I rented. I dreaded walking up the creaky staircase to my tiny room and my smaller life. Instead, I wandered past it up Second Avenue to 57th Street, to the gated and exclusive Sutton Place with its tall apartments and doormen. I strolled, or should I say stumbled, into the beautiful park in the middle of their pristine landscape. I walked through it, knowing what was on the other side—the East River.

I heard it before I saw it—small ripples and ice crunching into the shoreline, a tug boat chugging along out in the middle, barely visible with a sliver of the moon above. I wondered if the captain of that boat felt as lonely as I did, but at least he was going somewhere.

I perched myself on the wrought-iron fence and stared down into the black water. I had no money. I had no one to love.

I was headed nowhere. Large chunks of dirty ice floated by on their way to the sea, not a care in their world. I peered into the water, imagining what it would be like to have it close in around me, its coldness pulling me down into the dark. I wondered if anyone would miss me.

The high-pitched wail of fire engine in the distance shook my thoughts.

What am I doing?

I stepped down, turned up my collar, and headed home.

* * *

The last place I lived in The City, I paid $40 a month for a small room, with just a bed and dresser, but it had high ceilings, giving a sense of more space. Avery Willard, an edgy photographer, whose main client was Nat King Cole, rented me a room in his place. I kept waiting for the singer of *Nature Boy* and *Get Your Kicks on Route 66* to show up, maybe get an autograph, but it never happened—because Avery did his photography during the day while I worked at the bank.

* * *

With my love of the theater, I got to know all sorts of people. Bessie Winder was the wardrobe mistress for many Broadway musicals. At one opening, I stopped by the stage door, hoping to see her, dressed casually. Everyone else by the stage door was dressed to the nines and asking to see the stars.

The doorman asked if I was her friend and sent me up to the seventh floor where she was busy making last-second adjustment to all the costumes. I stood in a corner as she was a whirlwind of activity, custom-fitting gowns for the cast, a pin cushion around her left wrist, the right hand a blur, thimbles and scissors everywhere.

She let out a big sigh when they left the room for the opening acts, but was on call the rest of the night. After the show, we went out to some clubs where she had an "in." A nice way to spend an evening in New York City.

* * *

My parents visited me a few times during my time in The City. I felt like a tour guide, doing things with them I should have done before. We'd take in a play or musical, then do some cultural visits to a museum or monument. While Mother visited relatives one time, Dad and I went to see the Statue of Liberty. He was 50 years old and I just turned 26, but we both opted to climb the stairs to the top together.

"This is really something, Fred," he said, looking out over the harbor toward the City.

"I've seen it a few times at night with the torch all lit up. But yeah, it's really something, Dad."

* * *

Sailing with Bill Atwood in the Summer of 1947

After two years of working in The City, and having plenty of good times, I realized I wasn't getting anywhere—and would never make enough money working at the bank, not for what I wanted to do. It was time to go home and figure out where my life should go.

Buffalo, New York. A place where I spent a few months after the war and visited a few times during the holidays. Dad would sit in the living room and read the newspaper, or watch TV after his long hours at the A&P. Both my younger brother John and my sister Nancy were off at college. Mother had a room waiting for me and her stuffed pork chops ready to sizzle in a skillet. I'd had my fun in The City. It was time for me to grow up.

14

It was April 1948. I was 26 and back living with my parents in Buffalo, New York, actually Kenmore, an adjacent upscale town. There were twin beds and a dresser in my small bedroom, and a closet barely big enough to hold all my clothes. My younger sister Nancy was away at Alfred College, my younger brother John off on his own in an apartment, and my oldest brother Andy, Jr. still in D.C., so I had the run of the house and Mother's cooking.

There was still a little snow on the ground, but it was dirty and ready for a change, just like me. I missed the sounds and scents of New York City, the humanity on the subway, on the streets, in the clubs. It was all gone, only a quiet resignation filling its place.

I couldn't make it there.

I had no job and no plans. I never thought of the future. I only wanted to make up for my 3½ years of lost time in the Navy and go out for a few beers, some music, and laughs. I started a Christmas Club at a bank, but two months later pulled out all the money because I needed it for clothes or a good time.

I helped around home for a few months, mostly for Mother, trying to lighten her load—she appreciated it and doted over me a little. Over dinner, I'd get *looks* from Dad that told me he might be disappointed that I'm not involved in anything and have no plans, but he didn't say a word.

I finally saw an ad in the Buffalo Currier Express, a job opening as a bookkeeper at Buffalo Solvents and Chemicals. They distributed their products to industrial plants and hardware stores. I applied and the interview was simple. They were impressed that I worked in The City for two years at Chase National Bank in the foreign letters of credit department.

I became the assistant to the head bookkeeper, the fourth employee in the office. The rest of the employees included a driver and four men who worked out back in the warehouse. It was steady, simple work, and that was fine by me.

Buffalo Solvent and Chemicals. I'm 4th from the right in the back

I still didn't have a car and had no interest in driving. So, I took the bus and got rides from friends. At a luncheonette near work, I met Jerry, a guy who worked a block away from my company, and lived a few blocks from my parents' home. We hit it off—he had been in the Navy too, but in the Atlantic on a submarine. We swapped some war stories, me about natives, maggots, and torpedo juice, him about life as a bubble-head.

"Hey, you live so close, why don't I give you lift to work, Fred?" he asked.

"Sure. That'd be jake."

Just like that, we got into a nice pattern. He picked me up in the morning and drove me to work, then I'd usually would get a ride home from someone in the office.

Friday nights were my parents' night out. Mother would get her hair and nails done in the afternoon. They'd have cocktails at home before heading out to dinner at the Park Lane, a beautiful, big home that served upscale Italian fare. My parents were so well known, they had a table waiting for them and oftentimes the owner gave them a free round of drinks or desert.

For me, Friday nights meant coming home, making myself a sandwich, taking a shower, and changing clothes. I usually made myself a vodka tonic before going out, just to save a little money. Then I headed over to the Town Casino Nightclub, with its huge circular bar and big dining room. They knew me so well, I walked in like a king past the long line of patrons waiting to get in, then checked my coat, and took a seat at the bar. That is where I watched the shows and bought drinks for some of the chorus girls during their intermissions.

Sometimes before heading to the Town Casino, I stopped by the Buffalo Memorial Auditorium to watch professional wrestling matches, and see the likes of Gorgeous George with his huge mane of blond hair. His entrance was like nothing I'd seen before. A purple spotlight was on him when he strutted down the aisle toward the ring to the blaring sounds of *Pomp and Circumstance*. A beautiful ring girl preceded him, tossing red rose petals in front of him off a silver plate, George's sequined cape flapping behind him.

Buffalo Memorial Auditorium

Afterward, I found my spot at the Town Casino bar and listened to the likes of Sammy Davis Junior with the Will Maston Trio. I also got to hear Johnny Ray, Sophie Tucker, and Josephine Baker. I picked up an autograph from Danny Thomas who puffed on a huge cigar the whole time we talked.

Speaking of payday, my W-2 from 1949 shows I made $3,200 my first full year in the company—clearing around $50 a week. I wasn't paying any rent and didn't own a car, so my money went to clothes and good times. My bookkeeping job wasn't hard, just meticulous, and with such a small company, I got involved in all sorts of activities—even rolling up my sleeves to test chemical shipments in the lab. I dripped small samples in a vial, added a few drops of an exciter, heated it up, and made sure I saw the right colors.

During the week, I took my dinners at home. Mother, Dad, and I plopped in front of the television with our TV trays and watched Ed Sullivan or Milton Berle. Our meals were hearty and well balanced, like meatloaf with mashed potatoes and green beans. If it was nice outside, we ate on the patio—usually something like ham with potato salad.

One year blended into another. The Korean War started in 1950 and ended three years later. My older brother Andy got married on August 1, 1952, and I was his best man. My parents flew with me down to Washington, D.C. August in the capitol was insufferable with its heat and humidity. During the service at a Presbyterian church, I had to sneak into my suit pocket to get a handkerchief to wipe away all the sweat.

We stayed at the Wardman Park Hotel. It was old but beautiful. The dining room had a full band with a wonderful trio. As you'd imagine, I got to know them well during their breaks, buying them drinks at the bar. Since hotel entertainers weren't allowed in the pool area, I asked them to be my guest.

Three days of lounging by the pool with talented singers—my kind of place.

Later in 1952, Eisenhower got elected, the McCarthy Hearings were everywhere on the radio in May-June 1954, and I was back in D.C. in December of that year, my first niece Susan being born. I held the pink little bundle in my hands and was amazed—my brother Andy beaming like I'd never seen him. The looks I got from my family asked me, 'when will you find a girl, settle down, and start a family?'

I knew my answer then, but didn't say a word.

Never.

* * *

To me, my life wasn't monotonous at the time, but when I look back, it kind of feels that way. During the fall, I raked unending piles of autumn leaves until my hands got blisters. I helped Mother around the house. In the winters, I dug Dad's car out of the snow and got a smile. While my parents listened to the Yankees on the patio on summer days, I sprawled out on the lawn in the back yard with a transistor radio, immersed in the music of the day.

Every year, the owner of Buffalo Solvents and Chemicals took all the employees to the Buffalo Athletic Club for dinner. We dressed up. There were lots of speeches and awards for athletes, and overcooked chicken with some kind of sauce. Since I wasn't into sports, I listened passively to the bevy of speakers. I did get Joe DiMaggio's autograph (who I'll be mistaken for a few times in my life), but that was about it.

You might not know, but Buffalo was considered the windiest city in America, resting on the eastern shore of Lake Erie, and just a short ride from Niagara Falls. In the open walkway plaza off Main Street and next to City Hall, they crisscrossed ropes throughout the area to help keep pedestrians from blowing away from the harsh winter winds. If there was a little ice on the ground, people flew all over the place. I used those ropes more times than I want to remember.

Back at Buffalo Solvents and Chemicals, I continued to type invoices, and do reports when my boss dictated them. The company grew, moved into a large warehouse, and even got so big they add a railroad spur.

* * *

While *20,000 Leagues Under the Sea* filled movie screens across America, on January 4, 1955, I received an official certificate naming me the proud owner of Tract #D797173, Lot 243, in Dawson City, Yukon, Canada. As you can guess, I still have the certificate. I invested in the Klondike Big Inch Land Co., Inc. That's right—one square inch of land in Canada, in the gold rush area. I paid five dollars for the privilege to tell all of my friends that I had holdings in a Canadian gold field.

In 1955, I also bought some property in Vero Beach, Florida—and it wasn't a square inch. It was an official plot of land. I saw an ad in the Buffalo News. For only $245, I could be a land owner. Taxes that first year were $1.50. Twenty-six years later, I sold that piece of property for $3,000! (And, of course, I have copies of all the paperwork)

* * *

On a vacation to the City to catch a few plays and musicals, I stayed at the Algonquin Hotel, my favorite. Coming back from a Broadway show one night, I hopped on the elevator to find none other than Cesar Romero, accompanied by a tall, young, blond man—who could have been a model or an actor. I gave him a broad smile. "Hi. How are you?"

"Fine, thank you," he responded formally.

We rode together for a few floors. I tossed out a "Goodnight," as I exited the elevator. He simply nodded.

* * *

113

One memorable Thanksgiving meal showed the kind of playfulness our family could engage in. We had some friends over and Andy came up from Washington, D.C. with his wife Helen and their new baby Susan. After a few whiskey sours to get things going, we sat down for our traditional dinner. Mother passed her plate from the far end of the table and asked Father to serve her some creamed onions. He did, but splashed some on the table—which upset her no end. Later, when Father asked her for a roll, she picked one up and threw it at him. We all spent the next five minutes rolling on the floor laughing.

* * *

There was always something going on, even in Buffalo—especially with all the friends I made in the clubs I frequented. Tom, a buddy of mine, had a single-engine prop plane he kept out of the city in an old barn. One summer Saturday, he invited a group of us to join him for a party at the barn—an honest-to-god barn dance. It had everything—a live band, sawdust on the floor, and tables filled with food and liquor.

During the party, Barry took each of us up for a short flight. I still remember the rush, the wind mixed with the hot aromas of oil and gas as we soared over the fields.

He yelled over his shoulder at me. "Got your seatbelt on tight, Fred?"

I nodded back at him with a questioning look.

"Hold on!" he barked.

A barrel-roll. That's what he told me we did—after we landed. One thing I knew for sure, my stomach would always remember the name of that maneuver.

* * *

I dated a gal for a few years when I was in Buffalo, dark hair, tall—Rachel Catalano. Her last name was Italian, the living room furniture with its red velvet tufted couch covered in plastic told me just *how* Italian she was. I never met her Dad, but heard about him. Rachel and I did lots of dancing and she was the perfect party-going date. I met her mother a few times, the typical chubby wife of a mobster—I'm glad I never met him. When I moved to San Francisco, our dating ended.

* * *

In my ninth year with the company, Mr. Resch, the small aging owner, asked me into his office. "Fred, you're a good employee and do everything we ask of you, and do it well."

I received minor raises every year and heard a few atta-boys, so I wasn't sure where he was going with this. I leaned forward and nodded for him to continue.

"Fred, it's time we gave you a new title, and you'll pick up a few more duties." He coughed something into a handkerchief he always kept nearby. He always coughed. "It won't mean a raise right away." He eyed me over. "So, how would you like to see the title of Treasurer on your new business cards?"

"That would be nice, Mr. Resch. What more would you like me to do?"

He went over a few minor tasks, ones I could handle with little effort. But Treasurer? That was special.

Eight months later he died at his desk, most likely one last cough putting him down. A month after his funeral, I sat down with his son, David. He was more approachable than his father and we got along just fine.

"Dave," I began, "your father mentioned I'd be getting a raise some time after he gave me my new title."

"Yes, he did mention that to me." He broke eye contact with me and looked out the window. "Maybe we can look at this another time—later."

I'd been at Buffalo Solvents and Chemicals for ten years. I was 37 years old. It hit me—I was tired of cold Buffalo winters, stinking chemicals, and not getting a promised raise. This wouldn't be the first time in my life I did this.

I stood up, looming over him, placed my clenched fists on his desk, and gave him a big smile. "I quit."

15

It was May 1958. Two weeks passed since I quit Buffalo Solvents and Chemicals. I still got up early every morning, showered and shaved, trying to keep to some kind of normalcy. I wandered down to the kitchen, Dad already gone to work at the A&P, and found Mother by the sink, her head bowed— maybe crying. I never saw her cry before. I stepped back out of the room and let out a fake cough, walking in a few seconds later to find her apron at her eyes.

"What's for breakfast?" I asked, cheerfully.

Keeping her head away from me, she sniffled and moved to the fridge to grab milk and eggs. "Well, I was thinking French toast. Sound good, Fred?"

"Sure."

I sat at the kitchen table and scanned the Buffalo News Dad left behind, taking peeks at her from time to time.

"What a shame, looks like they discontinued the Packard," I tossed out.

"Those were nice," her voice trembles.

117

"And there's some new car coming out from Ford, called the Edsel. Kind of ugly."

"Hmm. Maybe your father will get one of those."

"I hope not."

The cast-iron skillet sizzled with a pat of butter she tossed in. She placed two slices of thick white bread into the egg mixture, then gently laid them in the hot pan. The aroma of hot butter, eggs, and cinnamon finally made it to my nose.

I turned a page and read a headline. "A lot going on these days. That satellite, the Explorer they launched in January, its batteries just ran out so it stopped sending more information. But, it says, they've learned a lot about what's going on in space. Even discovered something they call the Van Allen Radiation Belt."

"Your father says the Russians are way ahead of us."

She flipped the slices over in the pan and went to the cupboard for the Honey Bee Bear Syrup, placing it on the table. She rested her hand on my shoulder and looked down at the paper. She spotted a small article and pointed to it. "Looks like that Bobby Fischer's going to play chess in the international championship next year. My, and to think he's so accomplished at only fifteen years old."

Her words weren't meant to sting, but they did. There I was, 37 years old, without a job, no wife, no kids, no future, living with my parents.

"If I were younger, I might have joined Elvis in the Army."

That got a little chuckle out of her. She went back to the stove and stacked two hot slices of French toast on a plate, setting it down in front of me. "Orange juice?"

"Thanks, Mother."

* * *

I was lying on my bed and listening to the radio, surprised and awed by a new musical sound called *Vortex*. It started a few weeks before at the San Francisco Palladium during a concert featuring musicians who played bizarre rhythms on even stranger percussion pieces and created odd electronic sounds. There was something about it that mesmerized me. I thought back to the two times I was in San Francisco, preparing to go overseas in 1945, and then coming back in early 1946. The cool salt air. The friendly people. A night spent at the guard's shack at San Quentin Prison. The bars.

That's what I'll do.

Four days later, Mother and Dad drove me to the Buffalo Central Terminal train station, their car packed full of luggage containing all my clothes and a few mementos, a small black trunk lashed to the roof. I felt bad about leaving her alone in the house with Dad, their lives destined to fall into a dull pace, no children underfoot to distract them from their loneliness together. At least they'd have two grandchildren to visit out West.

"You take care now, Fred, and let me know if you need anything. And I mean anything," Mother said, hugging me. She shoved something into my coat pocket, and into my lapel she whispered, "Write me. Call me. Let me know how you're getting on."

"I will, Mother." I pulled away and saw tears in her eyes.

Dad tapped me on the shoulder and I turned to him.

He gave me a firm handshake. "Good luck, Fred."

I hopped aboard and waved back to them out the window of my Pullman car.

My third trip across America.

Half an hour after the train left the station, I gazed out at Lake Erie, ships and boats of all shapes and sizes dotted across the water—going somewhere, a purposeful destination in front of them. Canada was on the other side of the lake, a place I never cared to visit. Too cold. In fact, Buffalo was too cold. No future there, I knew that to be true now.

I reached in my pocket to find what Mother put there, an envelope with $500 cash and a letter.

You're really something, Mother.

Dear Frederick –

You are off on a marvelous journey, and a piece of my heart goes with you. Don't let your father or anyone else tell you that you must be anything more than you are. You are a fine man, in every respect. Do not measure yourself against your brothers or sister. Make your own life, Fred.

I would be disappointed to have your love of life fade as the years pass. I know what that's like. The money is from me, not your father—my rainy-day money I was saving for something special. That something special is you, Fred.

Take care. Write me, and call often.

Love, Mother.

The conductor knocked on my door and poked his head in. "Anything I can get you, sir?"

I cleared the lump in my throat. "Yeah. Where's the club car?"

On the train from Buffalo to San Francisco

* * *

Three days later, my train pulled into the Oakland terminal and I took the ferry across the bay, landing at the Ferry Building at the foot of Market Street in San Francisco. I got a porter to help me take all my luggage out to a cab stand. The cabbie

121

barely fit all my bags and trunk into his Yellow Cab. I hopped in the back seat. He flipped the meter handle down and shuffled with some papers on the seat next to him for a few moments. Finally, he looked into his rearview mirror and asked, "Where to?"

"The Plaza Hotel."

Ten minutes later, I'm checked into a gorgeous room on the tenth floor. I figured I could stay there a week before I found a more permanent place to live and find a job. At that moment, it was about getting cleaned up after my long trip and finding my way down to the hotel restaurant, then entertainment at a good bar.

* * *

Four days later, I answered an ad about a large, furnished studio apartment on Greenwich Street near Coit Tower. It had a small, clean kitchen and a full bath. The rent was $110 a month. I took it. The next morning, I moved in, tipping the cabbie extra for helping me bring in all my luggage.

I closed the door to my room and tossed the key in my hand, feeling the weight of it and what it meant. I looked around. A floor fan stood in one corner. A full bed pulled out of the sofa, four-drawer wooden dresser, a lamp on top of it with a pretty red shade, a small closet. On the window sill, a plant, maybe even a weed, nearly dead from lack of water. There was a black and white TV with rabbit ears. A print of a landscape hung over the headboard, most likely a Kansas farm with fields of harvested hay rolled into large bales.

It was after six o'clock by the time I washed up and changed my clothes. I stepped outside the front door of my apartment building and took in a deep breath of the city—it smelled like freedom and hope.

I looked up and down the street. It hit me how hungry I was. I walked down Greenwich street, and turned onto Grant Avenue for a few blocks until I found a coffee shop. Past that, there were restaurants and clubs, and further down was Chinatown. Later that night, I would find my favorite bar there, The Rickshaw.

* * *

A friend of my brother Andy lived in San Francisco and I looked her up. She suggested I check out Price Waterhouse for a job. I met Dominic Tarantino there and we talked about my background and jobs I might like. Dominic would become a lifelong friend. He advised me to go with him to apply for a job with the National Exhibition Company. We took the bus and trolley until we reached Seals Stadium, the current home and headquarters for the San Francisco Giants who just moved from New York.

My interview with them went well. I guess they liked that someone from Price Waterhouse vouched for me. That I worked at Chase National Bank in New York City, my stable employment at Buffalo Solvent and Chemicals, and that I'd been so meticulous in my tasks impressed them. I was hired on the spot into the accounting department to handle the bookkeeping and accouting needs of the organization.

Besides the twenty-five rostered players, there were all the coaches, scouts, managers, and a raft of support people, hundreds of employees—from ushers to ticket takers, even scoreboard operators. And there were the minor league clubs. The W-2s at the end of the year were endless.

That may sound like a lot of work, but it was nothing compared to Frank Bergonzi's load, the traveling secretary for the club. He was a little Italian guy who shook because he drank so much, and I understood why. He handled every aspect of the team's travels. Cabs. Buses. Hotels. Airplanes. Meals. Per diem for the players. Equipment and uniforms. Everything. When I saw him, he always had a cigarette in his mouth and rushing to somewhere.

* * *

The Giants played in Seals Stadium while Candlestick Park was being built for the opening of the 1960 season. Bill Rigney was the manager, and the team's roster had some famous players. I had to look them up because I never cared much about baseball. Willie Mays and rookie Orlando Cepeda were the stars and everyone clamored over them.

I met the team's head of scouting, Hall of Fame New York Giants left-handed pitcher Carl Hubbell. When he played, they used to call him *The Meal Ticket* because you could count on him to win so much. Nice guy, big hands, big laugh—his left arm crooked in a funny kind of way, like he was still ready to take the mound at any time. He talked a lot about baseball— stuff I never heard before, like about rookies and their five tools.

Seals Stadium

I spoke to Dad over the phone about my new job and he was not too happy. "The Giants, really? My god, Fred, don't you know the Yankees are the only team that matters?"

"Dad, I just work in the office. You know me, I'm not interested in attending any of the games. It's nice here. People are friendly." I paused, not knowing how he'd react. "You and Mother ought to come out and visit sometime. You know, maybe during the winter, especially when it gets so cold back there."

The phone went quiet on the other end. Finally, he cleared his throat. "Well, yes, she'd probably like that. And, Fred?"

"Yes?"

"Do you think you could get me an autographed picture of Willie Mays?"

"Sure, Dad."

There I was, on the other side of America, about as far away from my parents as I could get. I may have missed Mother's French toast and stuffed pork chops, but I was my own, doing good—and there were plenty of bars and nightlife waiting for me.

16

Baseball. *Take Me Out to the Ball Game* and *The Star Spangled Banner* were songs I never expected to hear eighty-one times a year for the next eighteen years—but that's what ended up happening. I didn't mind, really. After putting in a full day at the office writing checks, I'd wander into the press room just before game time to fill my plate from their lavish buffet. Deli meats and cheeses. Coleslaw and potato salad. Every kind of condiment on the planet. A full bar. Dessert trays with mini-éclairs, slices of carrot and German chocolate cake, pies—all there for the taking. I'd head to the press box to mingle with the writers and announcers from their cat-bird seats above home plate.

Russ Hodges and Lon Simmons were the radio and TV announcers during my first 13 years with the Giants. Russ' call of Bobby Thompson's home run, the *Shot Heard Round the World,* in the bottom of the ninth in 1951 to beat the Brooklyn Dodgers and win the pennant—that's the stuff baseball legend is all about. Russ had the smoothest voice, but that didn't help him when he died of a heart attack at only 61, right at the start of the 1971 baseball season. I felt real bad about that, and couldn't help but think of when I might pass, since I was 50 at the time. But I'm getting ahead of myself.

In late 1958, my parents shipped out my bed, dresser, and some other furniture—but most importantly, memorabilia from my childhood. The doctor's $55 bill from my botched tonsillectomy in 1928 when I was seven caught me by surprise. I set up a filing system to could keep track of the huge collection of paperwork—my school report cards, all my W-2's, Navy records, photographs, everything. It felt a lot more like home with my things around me, and with everything so organized.

Horace Stoneham in 1958

Horace Stoneham, the owner of the San Francisco Giants, was an incredible guy—always upbeat and with a big smile, nice "hellos" from him and his wife to everyone. That kept the organization humming and happy. It made my long hours pass by quickly. Even on Saturday and Sunday when the team played at home, I'd come in to oversee the time sheets for all the support personnel—groundskeepers, clubhouse crew, and ushers. I'd post them by hand to their payroll sheets—and I'd always pick up a good meal from the buffet during home games.

After a year in my apartment, I moved to a new place right across the street from Ghirardelli Square and its closed-down chocolate factory. From my second-floor window, I watched the comings and goings of so much of the city—the tourists, the locals, along with the strange and forgotten. San Francisco was changing right in front of me, yet the hippie movement that would change so much would be ten years away with its free love and drugs.

Two blocks from Fisherman's Wharf, and with a cable car a block east at Hyde and North Point Streets, I could get anywhere I needed easily. I felt so free—no car to learn how to drive or park, my will and the soles of my shoes were all I needed. I'd grab a brass trolley pole, hop aboard and let the fog, the scents of the wharf, and trolley bells whisk me away to small adventures. That's all I needed to make me happy, content to sightsee, and take in life on my own terms and time.

* * *

The Giants finished third out of eight teams in the National League in both 1958 and 1959, and I continued to explore more of the city, making a few friends along the way. The following year, I moved again—this time closer to downtown, near the corner of Leavenworth and Sutter Streets, only four blocks from Union Square. It was a cute place with a larger kitchen, and with lots of new restaurants and bars nearby to discover. I might have mentioned it already, but with being so busy at work, I didn't have much time to take in the nightlife, unless the Giants were out of town.

April 12, 1960 rolled around and the Giants played their first game in Candlestick Park. What a to do. The press box was filled with dignitaries, Vice-President Richard Nixon threw out the first pitch, and the Giants beat the Cardinals 3-1. It was a good start to a dull season that had us finish fifth, 16 games out of first place.

1960 San Francisco Giants Sluggers (Willie Mays on the far left)

* * *

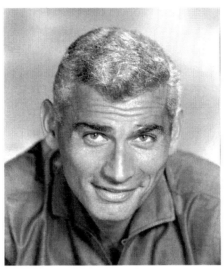

There were a few perks that came along with my job—like using the sauna at Candlestick Park after a long day of bookkeeping, usually when the team was on the road. The heat, the sweat, the dry air was so invigorating. Throughout my life, and my 18 years with the Giants, I ran into celebrities. I caught sight of movie star Jeff Chandler in the showers after he worked out with the club. He was nominated for a Supporting Actor Oscar playing Cochise in the 1951 move *Broken Arrow*. With him standing there in the buff, I was too embarrassed to ask him for an autograph.

* * *

My landlord owned a yacht and took me out a few times onto windy San Francisco Bay. The best part was seeing stark Alcatraz up close, and then Candlestick Park from the water—

the size of it and imagining the hundreds of people I knew who worked there.

My stay in this apartment ended when my landlord rented the room above me to a young woman—a very *active* young woman. Her squeaky bed and yelps of passion kept me awake at all hours. The Giants finished in third place in October, and in the middle of JFK winning the presidential election in November 1960, I moved into an old Spanish-style home up in the Twin Peaks area, occupying the penthouse apartment. What a view from the sun deck, all the way down to the bay.

I had my first adventure with a semi-pet in that apartment. I'd been there no more than a month when a little brown striped kitten scooted past my feet into my place when my hands were full of grocery bags. "Well, well, what do we have here?" I asked the critter. It shuffled over to me sideways and rubbed up against my legs, a throaty purr coming out.

A saucer of milk later and we were best friends. I called him Sammy. I never got a cat box, but instead let him go out onto the deck to do his business. That worked okay until one day I couldn't find him, but I kept hearing his *meow* from somewhere in the deck area. I went about making and eating my supper, but constantly went to check for him, calling out his name.

It was getting chilly, so I put on a sweater and grabbed a flashlight. An exhaust vent for the apartment below was just big enough for Sammy to crawl into. I pulled off the cover and shined my light down the shaft—and there he was probably four feet away. I reached down but arm wasn't long enough. "It's okay, I'll think of something," I told Sammy, then walked back into my apartment.

The thought of calling the fire department crossed my mind, but I wasn't about to give up. *What do I have that's long enough for me to grab him?* Nothing. Ah, but what if Sammy could grab onto something and I could get him out that way? Five minutes later, I lowered an old pair of gray slacks down the shaft and coaxed Sammy. "Grab onto it and I'll pull you out."

Wouldn't you know it, he did just that and I got him out. After a month, when I let him out the front door to go on one of his hunting expeditions, that was the last time I ever saw my Sammy.

* * *

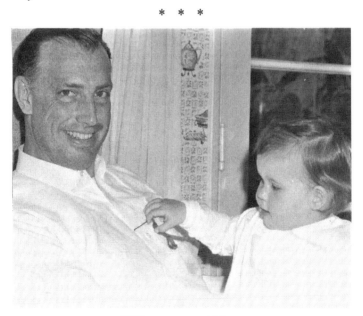

With one-year-old Sara

A year later, I became an uncle again. Sara Hillhouse was born on December 22, 1961. I was eager to see her, so I flew down to San Diego to visit my brother and his growing family over the holidays. Holding that small bundle of life in my hands, looking up at my 40-year-old reflection in the glass of the maternity ward window, I felt content with myself. I thought the experience might bring up some regrets of not marrying or having children, but I liked my life, the city I lived in, my work, and my friends. I was content.

Next—maybe learn to drive and get a car, possibly buy a house.

17

I didn't use the first of January each year to make resolutions about something I wanted to change in my life. I usually spent the night before at a nightclub with live music, taking a seat at the bar, sipping on a cold beer and taking in the show. Making resolutions isn't like me—I've always been pretty much happy with who I am and where I am.

From 1961-1963, I became a regular at a basement night club (I forget the name) on Leavenworth Street, a few blocks from where I lived. Singer Jack Jones (you might know him for singing the theme to the TV show *Love Boat*) was the headliner. We spent many an evening before his first show at the bar where I bought him screwdrivers and we chatted. Great guy. Incredible voice.

* * *

The start of 1962 found me gearing up for a new baseball season and all the work ahead. Spring training was a month away and hundreds of seasonal staff would be joining the San Francisco Giants. The past year, the team finished third out of eight teams, a disappointment to our first year manager, but there was always new hope every year for what the team could be. Alvin "the Swamp Fox" Dark was only 40 and in his second season managing the team. He had a great southern Louisiana drawl with words and expressions I'd never heard before, like *tammy shoes* for sneakers. I liked him, but more importantly, the players did.

Nineteen sixty-two brought changes to baseball: First, two new teams were added to the National League, the Houston Colt .45s, and the New York Mets; and, Second, the number of games expanded from 154 a year to 162. That translated to much more check writing for me.

In the front office, Carl Hubbell was more excited than ever about the team he put together with his scouting organization. Willie Mays, the *Say Hey Kid*, was still a spry 31 years old and a perennial all-star, Orlando Cepeda just came off a great year, and huge Willie McCovey was crushing baseballs with his tremendous left-handed swing. The pitching staff had two young pitchers, Juan Marichal and Gaylord Perry, who looked like they might be coming into their own. The two "Billys" were supposed to anchor the staff. That'd be Billy O'Dell and Billy Pierce, coupled with steady Jack Sanford.

Meanwhile, I was well-situated in my penthouse apartment in an older home in the Twin Peaks area, paying $150 a month rent, and taking in the sun on my huge 400-square-foot deck whenever the fog allowed. I would end up staying in that apartment five years, and probably would have kept living there had the owners not decided to tear it down and build a large apartment complex.

A lot was going on in 1962. *West Side Story* won the Oscar for Best Picture, the song of the year was *Moon River*, John Steinbeck won the Nobel Prize for Literature, Marilyn Monroe died, and Johnny Carson took over as host for The Tonight Show. But this baseball season was special. My Giants had two remarkable first months of the season and we were in first place, but then the Dodgers took off on a huge winning spurt. During the dog days of August, the Cuban Missile Crisis was going on, but I didn't notice, because the San Francisco Giants were in second place, trailing the Dodgers who appeared as if they might run away with the pennant.

After 161 games, it all came down to the final day of the season. My Giants trailed the Dodgers by a single game. We played the Houston Colt .45s at home, while the Dodgers played the St. Louis Cardinals in Los Angeles. We watched the Dodgers' scoreboard all game long—everyone on the edge of their seats. The press box kept switching over to the Dodgers' broadcast while watching our game. I hardly touched my pastrami sandwich and potato salad, so engrossed in the drama.

Willie Mays with Manager Alvin Dark

Finally, in the eighth inning, Willie Mays hit a towering two-run homer. As crazy and excited as everyone got, we had to settle down and wait until the last out of the ninth inning. We won the game 2-1 and the stadium erupted in a celebration like I never heard or saw before. But then everyone quieted down while we awaited the final score of the Dodgers' game. If they won, they would play the NY Yankees in the World Series. If they lost, we'd have to play them in a divisional playoff series. So much rode on the outcome of their game, we listened intently to Vince Scully's call.

The Dodgers were in the midst of a pitchers' duel until Gene Oliver, the catcher for the Cardinals, hit a line drive home run off Johnny Podres in the eighth inning. Everyone in

Candlestick went crazy—but then had to settle down again to hold our collective breaths for the next inning-and-a-half.

The Dodgers didn't score in the eighth and neither did the Cardinals in the top of the ninth. In the bottom of the ninth inning, the first Dodger batter flew out, the next hit a line-drive out, and their *final* batter popped up to second base! Now Candlestick Park could erupt—and did it! Everyone grabbed each other and danced around, hats flying in the air.

I walked down to the clubhouse and stood in the doorway, not wanting to get my suit drenched in champagne. The last time I saw guys celebrate that hard was back in Guam on New Years' Eve 1946—then I was headed home from Okinawa on my way to finish up 1,225 days in the Navy.

Our manager, Alvin Dark, held up his hands to calm everyone down—his uniform soaked clear through with bubbly. He yelled above all the ruckus in his Louisiana accent, "Hey, y'all, let's settle down now. Settle down."

The room got quiet, except for the *pop* from a fresh champagne bottle somewhere.

"We got us a three-game series against the Dodgers comin' up."

Someone in the back of the room yelled, "We'll kill 'em!"

Everyone busted up until Alvin held up his hands again. "Yes, that's what we'll do, alright. But as my daddy from used to say, 'By talking too loud, the jaw becomes swelled.' In the next three days, we're gonna do some talking—but it's gonna be with our bats, our arms, our gloves, and our legs. Come see now."

All twenty-five players and coaches swarmed in around him, their arms reaching for the center of the room. Someone yelled out, each word louder than the previous. "One. Two. Three."

Everyone shouted, "WIN!"

Their hands flew in the air, followed by lots of slaps on the back, then it was time for business. Everyone walked back to their lockers with a quiet knowing—they had to win two games in the next three days. If they did that, the San Francisco Giants would be in the World Series to face their dreaded rival, the New York Yankees.

The first game against the Dodgers was in Candlestick Park the very next day, October 1, 1962, at 2:39 in the afternoon. The twenty-five players on the roster got themselves mentally prepared, especially our starter for the game, Billy Pierce. He was set to face Sandy Koufax, one of the hardest throwing left-handed pitchers in baseball history. Mid-morning, I poked my head in the clubhouse to find Alvin Dark going over Koufax's approach to batters with all our players, the coaches tossing in tips.

Then it was back to my office. Everyone in the organization scrambled to call in extra help from every corner of San Francisco—ushers, the ticket office, food service, suppliers. I knew I'd be writing checks for all the players and their expenses, but it didn't matter, because we were going to the World Series—if we could beat the Dodgers. The additional buzz in the office was incredible, not only about the team, but what it would mean for year-end bonuses for everyone. We usually got a one or two-month bonus, but with the World Series, that would mean a whole lot more.

We took the first game against the Dodger 8-0, a surprise to everyone in baseball. The next game in the Dodgers' new stadium in Los Angeles was different. We led 5-0 in the sixth inning and thought it was over until the Dodgers came back with seven runs. We ended up losing 8-7, forcing the third and final game. I watched that game in the office with some of the other personnel who were left behind. We were losing 4-2 going into the ninth inning. But somehow, in the top of the ninth we got four walks sprinkled in between three hits, a sacrifice fly, and wild pitch, and we led 6-4 going into the Dodgers' last chance in the bottom of the ninth. Three up. Three down. We were going to the World Series!

The Yankees. The New York Yankees! The Giants and Yankees matched off six times before in the World Series, but those were all in New York, the *Subway Series*—and the Yankees won the last four meetings, most recently 11 years before in 1951.

This year's Yankees lineup was ferocious, anchored by Mickey Mantle and Roger Maris, the duo who pounded out 115 home runs between them the year before, Roger Maris getting his 61st homer on the last day of the season to surpass Babe Ruth's record of 60. Mickey was considered so dangerous to opposing pitchers, that he led the league in walks in 1962. I had to look up all this because I wasn't really that much into baseball, but that all changed this year.

The first game against the Yankees was the day after we beat the Dodgers to win the National League Pennant. The Yankees got three days off during our battle against the Dodgers, so their players and pitchers were well rested. Not so for us. Whitey Ford, their All-Star pitcher threw the whole game first game, while my Giants used three pitchers. The game was tied 2-2 until the 7th inning, and then the Giants' wheels fell off, finally losing 6-2. Our players looked worn out on the field—so much taken out of them the three days before against the Dodgers.

The next day, my Giants regrouped and Jack Sanford pitched a three-hit shut-out. He held the powerful Yankees scoreless! We got a run in the first inning, and then Willy McCovey launched a home run to deep right field in the 7th inning. We won 2-0.

I know I keep going on about the Giants, but 1962 was magical. It would be 27 years until the Giants won the pennant and made the playoffs again, so even in looking back, it held so much significance.

Sadly, the Giants lost the third game of the series, playing in New York, in a close 3-2 score, unable to overcome the Yankees three runs in the 7th inning, but made it interesting with two runs in the ninth. I never traveled with the team, staying in San Francisco busy writing checks for all the expenses the Giants incurred with the Dodgers' playoff games and the two World Series Games. But that didn't keep me from being glued to the TV with some of the other office staff.

The fourth game, we crushed the Yankees 7-3, getting a grand slam out of our second baseman Chuck Hiller—who hit only three home runs all year. The fifth game was a real nail-biter. We were tied 2-2 going into the eighth inning until the Yankees scored three runs. We countered with one the next inning, but not enough to lose 5-3.

Back to Candlestick Park and home cooking, the sixth game, and a must-win for the Giants—Monday, October 15. We pounced on the Yankees with three runs in the fourth and two more in the fifth—and held them to one run each in two other innings to win 5-2.

Three wins each and we were on to the 7th and final game of the World Series. The press room was packed, the buffet the best it'd ever been. I loaded up my plate and took in everything, savoring a mound of roast beef from a carving station. The Yankees scored one run in the fifth inning and it stayed that way until the ninth when the Giants finally put together a rally. Matty Alou's lead-off bunt between first and second got it going, but the next two batters struck out. Then Willie Mays hit a double with Alou held up at third. The crowd had been holding their breath all game and now everyone stood and yelled at the top of their lungs.

Even the reporters and announcers in the press box got on their feet when big Willy McCovey stepped to the plate. Four pitches later, McCovey let loose a monstrous swing, the ball scorched low toward right field—but Yankees second baseman Bobby Richardson snagged it for the last out.

We lost. The game over. I never experienced a stadium's let down like that, a low, collective groan followed by appreciative clapping for such an incredible season.

Everyone in the press box paused for a second before they jumped back on their typewriters and phones, either writing their final recap of the game or calling it into their newspapers.

I wandered back to my office to await the tallies coming in from each of the departments with their time sheets for everyone on their payrolls. The muffled voice of the public address announcer thanked everyone for coming out to the game. The organist played her final song, like a funeral dirge, capping off a long, remarkable, yet disappointing season. Next year. There's always next year.

I sharpened a number two pencil, straightened my desk, pulled out my ledgers, and waited.

18

Horace Stoneham, the Giants owner was especially generous with our Christmas bonuses in 1962. I should know, I wrote all the checks—for management and all the office staff. Before our playoff and World Series appearance, our yearly bonus was usually a month's pay. That year it was two months! I celebrated extra hard that New Year's Eve. I can't recall what nightclub (or clubs) I went to because I partied so much, but I do remember it was fun.

Bill Brandt, my boss with the Giants, came from New York with the club. He was a thick man in every aspect—thick hands, face, hair, and body—and a chain smoker. A carton of unfiltered Luckys always sat on his desk next to a massive amber ashtray that I never saw empty. A huge safe stood on the wall behind me. When I would hand him a pile of checks to sign, he'd pick up his pen and go to work.

* * *

I almost forgot, my parents came out to see me early in 1963 in the dead of winter like I suggested. Even though it was foggy, a little windy, and chilly in my new city, it was nothing compared to the frozen tundra of Buffalo. They stayed four days and I showed them around. Their first night, I wanted to take them to one of the fish restaurants by the wharf, but Dad insisted on getting a steak.

When they visited my apartment, Dad plopped in my easy chair to watch the Yankees on TV while I showed my mother around. When she came into my room, she sighed deeply, and paused to take it all in. She moved around the room slowly, lightly touching my furniture, as if she wanted to leave a part of herself behind, but also I think to remind herself that her son was settled in.

She turned and looked at me in only the way a concerned mother can. "This is so nice. You're happy here, aren't you, Fred?"

"Yes, this move to San Francisco has been good for me."

Dad let out a yelp from the living room, "Oh, come on, ump—know your strike zone!"

I ushered my mother back into the living room, that unanswered question to remain just that for the rest of our lives.

The next day, I took them out to Candlestick Park where I gave them a tour of the place.

"This is really something, Fred. Really something."

That was a lot coming from Dad. I could tell they liked my new city. When they left for San Diego, for first time in my life, my mother didn't slip some money into my hand or a coat pocket.

In San Diego was my older brother Andy and his family who moved there a few years before. This would be the first of yearly visits from my parents, and as you can imagine, an excuse to come to the West Coast to visit me and Andy and their grandchildren.

* * *

To get more involved in the San Francisco scene, I joined a monthly dining group—trying out new restaurants, always new adventures. The curry dishes at the India House with Pimms Club drinks was a favorite. We tried out an Armenian restaurant on Union Street with its pillows on the floor and all courses eaten without utensils—only our fingers. On one outing, we traveled to Napa Valley for a picnic at the Lewis M. Martini Winery. A full four-course meal with grilled steak and select wines with each course. The meal ended with tiramisu for desert with the Mountain Zinfandel Vintage 1968 poured by none other than Mr. Martini himself.

After the '62 season, I had business cards made. "Fred Hillhouse, Accounting" in raised letters next to the San Francisco Giants logo. Classy. When I met entertainers at bars and bought them drinks, or went to my barber or clothier, they'd eventually get around to asking me what I did. Without saying a word, I'd reach into my wallet and hand them a card. It was always fun to watch their eyes light up, some with envy.

A common question was, "Fred, do you think maybe you could get me into the clubhouse, you know, to meet some of the Giants?"

I'd play along. "Sure, let me see what I can do. Any players in particular?"

Everyone had their favorites, but Willie Mays always topped their list, followed by big Willie McCovey, Orlando Cepeda, Juan Marichal, and Felipe Alou. I don't remember taking anyone to a game, but I did get them a few autographs.

Speaking of autographs, I signed some for fans. What? You don't believe me? A few times while I stood next to Carl Hubbell talking, or once when I traveled with the team when we visited San Quentin Penitentiary, people came up to me and asked, "Joe, can I get your autograph?" They thought I was Joe DiMaggio!

Not wanting to be dishonest, I'd usually say, "Sorry, but I'm not Joe." They didn't care. They assumed because I was with Carl Hubble, I was someone famous, so I'd sign my name.

At six-feet, two inches and thin like Joe DiMaggio, I kind of had his look. Can you see why they might have thought so? Carl Hubbell got a kick out of that.

I forgot to mention, during a trip to New York City in the mid-50's, I was taking a cab to the Algonquin Hotel, a favorite place of mine to stay. When we pulled up, the cabbie looked at me confused and said, "Don't you want to go to Yankee Stadium, Mr. DiMaggio?"

I got a kick out of that.

If you wondered, that's Joe on the left and me on the right! One of the many major difference between us was that he married Marilyn Monroe. After she died in 1962, I heard he went to her grave every week and left a bouquet of roses. I wish I could have felt that way about someone.

* * *

There were very high hopes going into the 1963 season, since most of our World Series players were still on the roster, and with the same ownership and management in place. The Giants were expected to repeat. My big accomplishment, at the ripe age of 42, was to stop relying on the trolley, buses or co-workers to give me rides, but instead to get my own wheels. Austin Tinsley gave me more lifts back and forth to work than I wish to remember. He was the driver for Horace Stoneman, the team's owner, and we got on just fine.

Since I didn't think I could afford a car, I spotted something else in a showroom window. A Lambretta Scooter.

For that I wouldn't need a license, and back then there were no laws requiring riders to wear helmets. To convince me I could handle the scooter, the salesman loaded the Lambretta into the back of his truck and drove us to a nearby park. There he showed me how to start it up, use the clutch and gas, shift gears, and most importantly, how to stop. Since I was already comfortable riding a bicycle when I was a kid, this brought back lots of memories and a sense of freedom I'd left behind.

My Lambretta was a soft light blue and perfect for getting around the city, but I did my best to avoid the steep hills with their severe inclines. I zipped all over San Francisco on my Lambretta. I had a few pictures taken and sent one to my mother with a card. "Look mother, I'm finally driving!"

I got a phone call from her right away, her worry always the glue that held our family in place. After I appeased her concerns for my safety, it was time for more wind in my hair and sun on my face.

The 1963 Giants never pulled away from the other nine National Teams, but we were in first place by half a game on June 24. As it would turn out, that would be our last lead. We faded "down the stretch" as they call it, finishing third in the league, eleven games out of first place.

That didn't bother me much, because I could go anywhere on my scooter. That opened up new places to visit around the city, although I never drove at night.

There was a basement bar on Broadway and Grant that had a slide, kind of like a chute, that I'd take to get into the place. I always found a good spot by the bar to the watch the women in their dresses come flying down. What a show!

We were in the off-season when JFK was assassinated in November 1963. I could not imagine what it would have been like to host a baseball game in the midst of such tragedy. I was at work that day when the news hit. The office became too quiet—the staff and secretaries huddled in small groups, some crying, many completely unable to work. I felt a loss unlike anything I had in my life, a hollow emptiness filling me. I couldn't help but wonder what was happening to this country of mine. The Company gave us the next week off to mourn.

* * *

The Giants' 1964 season had us in first place on July 20, but again that was as far as we went. We ended that season in fourth place, but only three games out of first, the disappointment felt by everyone.

For a while, I enjoyed $50 haircuts at a fancy place off Union Square on Maiden Lane. Why the high price, especially with my hair thinning? It was the extras. They gave a full wash and dry, served champagne, hot towels, and a perfect straight-razor shave. That kept me looking good with my ever-expanding wardrobe. I took advantage of clothes sales—like when Roos Atkins Men's Clothiers had a buy-one, get the second for a penny sale on sports coats for Washington's birthday. I bought a green one, just like they handed out for the Masters' Golf Tournament winner each year, and a blue one just for fun.

In the 1965 and 1966 seasons, we finished in second place, only two games out of first. That was tough on everyone as well, the let-down for some of the players very difficult. That was one of the only times I ever saw grown men cry.

I kept recording expenses in ledgers, writing payroll checks, and taking advantage of the incredible buffet in the pressroom 81 times a year when the team played their home games.

1967 brought with it significant changes in my life—my first car and my first pet! After four years on my scooter, sometimes in the unfriendly weather of San Francisco (even riding across the Golden Gate Bridge a few times), all it took was spotting a discount offer for driving lessons and I signed up. I needed an extra lesson, seven in all, to master the clutch, accelerator, gear shift, and brakes.

Harold, the instructor, kept telling me, "Fred, you're doing just fine." All the time he tried to build up my confidence when

I drove, but out of the corner of my eyes I watched him tense up, ready to grab hold of the steering wheel or slam on the brakes on his side of the dual-controlled car.

My biggest challenge was stopping in the middle of one of San Francisco's well-known hills, like Gough Street. I tried several times to step on the gas quickly while I let out the clutch, but I kept stalling the car. Finally, I pleaded, "Harold, you've got to get us off this hill. I just can't do it."

Harold took over the controls on his passenger seat and I let out a big sigh. I watched his feet work the pedals and his left hand ease off the parking brake. Not even an inch did we roll backwards—amazing.

Arthur Schultz, ticket manager for the Giants, had a VW Bug as well. He let me borrow his car so I could practice, driving around the Candlestick Park parking lot. I put a lot of miles on his vehicle.

Since my training vehicle was a VW Bug, it only made sense that I buy one. I negotiated a $150 trade-in for my Lambretta and put $350 cash down. I financed the balance through Wells Fargo—$2,099 for my Zenith Blue convertible VW Bug for thirty-six months at $70.58 a month. As you might expect, I studied hard for the DMV test and passed on the first go-round. Oh, and I still have the paperwork for the loan.

After settling into my new car, on a whim, I bought a cute Boston Terrier—reminding me of the pet dog I had as a kid. I named him Brandy, and it didn't take him long to be house-broken. He loved to pose for pictures and was a hit everywhere I took him on our walks around the neighborhood, city, and the ballpark office on weekends.

Brandy

* * *

Again, running into celebrities became one of my favorite past times. At the height of the popularity of the TV show

Gilligan's Island, I was getting my glasses adjusted at my optometrists, a lovely lady walked in and sat down next to me. It was none other than Natalie Schafer, known as Thurston Howell III's wife Lovey. What a delightful woman, in town for a play she starred in.

On a weekend trip to Los Angeles to take in Universal Studios, I stayed at a nearby motel. Standing at the reception desk one night, but who should sidle up to me but Aldo Ray, the actor. He usually played cops or soldiers. We had a most delightful chat talking about our experiences in the Pacific during WWII—he as frogman, me a pharmacist. I asked him what brought him to the motel bar.

"I'm staying here, waiting for my divorce to be finalized." He pointed up toward the Hollywood hills. "She's up there with my house."

* * *

Through my friends, the Littlefields, I met Paula Haller, who became a special companion. She was a docent at the Asia-Pacific Museum in Golden Gate Park. The museum engaged a Tea Master from Japan to demonstrate their tea ceremony. Paula was so taken with him, that she invited him and three geisha assistants for lunch at her home, and included me as her guest. The pomp and colorful costumes made the afternoon delightful. For lunch, we dined on three elegant courses, the most notable was artichokes. She had to demonstrate how to peel off a leaf, dip it in drawn butter or mayonnaise, then place it in our mouths and scrape off the artichoke meat from the leaves. An unusual experience for certain—and I never had it again.

* * *

As a team, the 1967 Giants were never once in first place during the season, finishing a distant second to St. Louis, who went on to beat the Boston Red Sox in seven games in the World Series.

All four Hillhouse children went to Boca Raton for my parents' 50th wedding anniversary in 1967. Andy took old photographs from when they were married in 1917 and enlarged them for the event, stationing them at each side of the entrance to the grand ballroom we rented at the Boca Raton Country Club.

We ended our late afternoon affair with a private family dinner. I looked over at Dad as he attacked his prime rib and baked potato, while my mother picked at her sea bass, a pallor of gray over her. Three years later all four Hillhouse children would come back to Boca, but for one of the saddest days of my life.

From left to right around the table:
Andy and his wife Helen, John, Nancy, me, and our parents

* * *

In 1968, the team switched managers, and I moved into another apartment about a mile away from where I currently lived, over near the corner of 21st Street and Sanchez. It would have been great except that the two guys who lived above me stomped around in their work boots at all hours. My stay there lasted only a few months.

A week before the season started, on April 4, 1968, Martin Luther King, Jr. was assassinated in Memphis, Tennessee. Everywhere in the city, you could feel the tension. Rumors flew around the office about adding security for our opening game on April 10, and getting escorts for the players. No one understood what might happen next.

My Giants were in first place on June 1, but that would be the last time. Four days later on Wednesday morning, June 5, 1968, I took Brandy for our usual morning walk. Everywhere I went, people huddled together and cried. I had to ask. Between her sobs, a gray-haired lady with a cane told me that Robert Kennedy had been shot in early in the morning in the kitchen of a hotel in Los Angeles. All I could wonder was, *Has this country gone completely crazy?*

There was a moment of silence that afternoon before the Giants' game against the Phillies. Just over 3,000 people, the smallest in history, watched the Giants lose 2-1. There was a dark cloud over every aspect of the game, the press box unusually quiet, the announcers stunted in their call of the play-by-play.

I drove home, took Brandy for a walk, and came back to our apartment where I sat in the dark, eventually dozing off in my easy chair. While most of the world slept like me, Bobby Kennedy was pronounced dead at 1:44 am on June 6, 1968.

* * *

1969 brought all kinds of changes to baseball—four new teams were added, two each to the National League and American League, which then split into two divisions, an east and west. Worst of all for us, the Oakland Athletics took up residency in the bay area. With our season ticket sales dwindling, along with our attendance, male staff personnel took a twenty-five percent pay cut. I guess they figured the ladies got paid too little anyway. That pay cut hurt my social life more than anything else. Some of the bartenders I became friends with empathized and let me run up a little tab.

Even with Willie McCovey slugging 45 home runs and being named the National League Player of the Year, it wasn't enough for my Giants to win the pennant—although they tried. The last time we were in first place was with a week remaining in the regular season on September 22.

I couldn't believe that the Miracle Mets beat the Atlanta Braves for the National League title and then went on to win the World Series against the Baltimore Orioles. I actually watched the games, unusual for me. Maybe I was becoming a baseball fan.

* * *

During my parents' trip to visit me that year, my mother asked, "Are you smoking now, Fred?"

I looked at the long ash hanging from her Kent and shook my head. "No."

"Then why do your clothes smell like smoke?"

I explained. She bought me a small fan which I placed on Bill Brandt's desk, pointing at him and his ashtray. I enjoyed watching him blink his eyes with all the smoke billowing in his face. It kept our meetings brief.

* * *

1970 was even worse for my Giants—but not for me. They were never in contention, and finished third, sixteen games out of first. During the off season, I bought a home. For $30,000, I purchased a handsome custom-built, two-bedroom, two-bath house on 430 Hazelwood Avenue off of Monterey Boulevard near Mt. Davidson Park. It sat on a corner on a little rise with a view looking west. White stucco, gray pitched slate roof, fireplace with a heavy wood mantle, built-in buffet in the dining room with a mirror backing.

To make it all happen, I asked the team's Vice President of Operations if I could borrow $5,000.

"Sure," was his answer. "And Fred, just take something out of each paycheck to pay it back."

I put $3,000 down on my first home, spent another $1,000 on furniture and appliances, and I was in my new place with a little left over for savings. So, Brandy and I moved in. Now I also had a place for my parents to stay when they visited each year.

Sunday champagne (sparkling cider) brunch with Brandy

taBrandy and I got in our morning and evening walks at the nearby park. With him around, I didn't go out as much to nightclubs, preferring to stay inside our new home together. I finally found a best friend and a home to share.

* * *

Nineteen-seventy ended on such a sad note. My mother died after a long battle with cancer just six days before Christmas, two weeks after I turned 49. My three siblings and I flew back Boca Raton for her open casket funeral, sequestered off in a side room so that other guests couldn't see us grieve. We were there for our father during this difficult time. I looked at my brothers and sisters during the service, and could almost see the precious memories we each carried of our mother in their eyes.

L to R: John, me, Dad, and Andy

Of all the things that weighed on me about her death, what upset me most was the way the pastor kept referring to her as "Mrs. Hillhouse" all through the service.

Her name was Ednah. She made a hole in one and I was there. She died of lung and liver cancer—from a lifetime of smoking and drinking. She took me to dance lessons, and she never told me why she cried. She was my mother.

19

Nineteen seventy-one was not without incident in my adopted home city of San Francisco. In January, the thick bay fog caused two tankers to crash and spill 1.9 million gallons of oil just west of the Golden Gate Bridge. In June, the FBI and federal marshals took back Alcatraz from a small group of armed American Indians. The movie *Dirty Harry*, which was shot in the city, came out that year—and 320 hippies from San Francisco formed a commune they called The Farm on 1,750 acres in Lewis County, Tennessee. San Francisco definitely had become a beacon for social change in America.

Willie Mays turned 40 years old one month into the 1971 season, and I reached the ripe age of 50 later in the year. He got paid $160,000 for hitting towering homeruns and my salary was $4,100 for adding up numbers and writing checks. What a season that was for the Giants, making it into the playoffs for the first time in nine years.

* * *

I also got a second dog, Angus, a Terrier mix. He and Brandy quickly became best friends and I delighted watching them romp around my upstairs living room or in my downstairs rec room. Every time I asked, "Want to go for a ride?", they twirled around in circles, yipping in happiness.

Angus

I draped a multi-colored afghan over the back seat of my VW for them. They loved looking out the small side windows and lapping up the scents of the city from the open front windows. On sunny days, I'd put the convertible down and the looks we'd get from other drivers and pedestrians was priceless—instant friends wherever we went.

I had a big back yard that needed lots of work. Always good at raking leaves and mowing the lawn at my parents' home, fixing up my own yard was different. I went to local nursery and was recommended to buy fuchsia plants. Well, I bought one, then another, then joined a fuchsia club. Two guys who ran the club helped me build a redwood-beamed arbor where I hung the baskets. They took a lot of work, needing to be re-potted every year. And then there were the white flies and their incessant attacks. To keep them in check, I sprayed them with a mixture of soap, water, and rubbing alcohol. By the time I would move to San Diego in 1976, I had a collection of over 100 fuchsias, but only took a handful with me.

* * *

Another celebrity encounter ended up giving me a headache. In an April pre-season game, I wandered into the Stadium Club, a very fancy place reserved for season ticket holders. Sitting at the long bar was none other than the singing cowboy, Gene Autry. I sidled up to him and said hello.

"Join me for a drink, will you, Fred," he commanded with a smile. "I'm drinking screwdrivers."

After four drinks, I gave up—but he kept going. One of the nicest men I ever met.

* * *

What a year 1972 was. My San Francisco Giants took over first place in the National West seven days into the new season on Monday, April 12, and never looked back. We ended up edging out the rival L.A. Dodgers by just one game to end the season.

Bobby Bonds, who came to the team as a rookie only three years before, took over as our home run king, belting 33 home runs, while Willy McCovey and Willie Mays added 18 each. We had a strong group of young sluggers on the bench as well— Dave Kingman, who would crush home runs for eight different teams during his career, and George Foster, who found fame with the Cincinnati Reds.

On weekends when the Giants played out of town, I brought Brandy and Angus to the office with me and they became immediate hits with everyone. I can't begin to guess how many photos were taken of them, and with them. My coworkers treated Brandy like the king he was, and Angus as his young prince.

Charlie Fox, who took over managing the team during the previous season, kept the clubhouse loose and fun, probably one of the reasons the team did so well. After the season ended, all we had to do was win three games against the red hot Pittsburgh Pirates and we'd be back in the World Series, a place we hadn't been in nine years. Without saying the words, everyone wanted these games extra hard, knowing Willie Mays was nearing the end of his career, having missed 16 games during the regular season due to injuries.

We played the first game at home and won 5-4, Gaylord Perry pitching a complete game, and Willy McCovey putting one out to help in the win.

Our next home game we lost 9-4 even though Willie Mays slugged a homer. Then it was off to Pittsburgh where we needed to win at least one game to bring the series back to San Francisco.

Two lone home runs off of our all-star pitcher, Juan Marichal, was enough for the Pirates to beat us 2-1 and make it a do-or-die situation for game four the following day on October 6th.

That game, we were tied 5-5 going into the Pirates' bottom of the sixth, with big Willy McCovey putting one over the wall earlier to keep us in the game. However, the Pirates got four runs in the bottom of the sixth and we didn't respond with any more runs.

I sat with other staff members huddled around a black and white TV in the office at Candlestick Park, all sharing in the stunned heartbreak of coming so close to returning to the World Series.

With my head down, I got in my VW bug and went home. When I walked in to find Brandy and Angus so happy to see me, the Giants' heartbreaking loss melted.

* * *

Speaking of the Giants office staff, I became the regular dance partner for Mary, a 40s redhead who worked as the secretary for the club's Vice President, Chub Feeney. She loved to spin around on the dance floor, and we found ourselves going out once in a while to different clubs with small combos who still played the music of my youth. The Palace Hotel was our favorite. She appreciated all the lessons I took from the Steele sisters when I was 14, thirty-six years before—and my feet hadn't been that happy in years.

The 1972 season was the saddest one ever, and not because we finished fifth, twenty-six and a half games out of first place, and that there were only four teams in all of baseball with worse records. It was because the team traded Willie Mays to the New York Mets. The Giants was the only team Willie played for in his entire career, since 1951. Trading him away was treason.

I don't know how many times I got asked the question, "Why? Why did you trade Willie?" Strangers and bartenders, all fans for so many years—shared their anger and disappointment with me. Brandy, Angus, and I kept to our home more often after that, and handing out my San Francisco Giants business cards became less a source of pride.

Cutting a rug with Helen, Andy's wife

* * *

Walking down Geary Street, I had one of the most delightful celebrity sightings—Miss Bette Davis, such a petite woman, doing some window shopping with a friend. You never realize how tall someone is when they're on the big screen. I recalled one of her famous quotes, "Old age is for sissies."

I couldn't help but bow slightly and say, "Enjoyed your show, Miss Davis."

She returned a gracious smile and a small nod. "Why, thank you."

I continued walking on, an extra bounce in my step from the encounter.

* * *

Me and my sister Nancy during a visit in 1974

The following four seasons were without any success by the Giants, finishing third, fifth, third, and fourth. Before the 1976 season began, management decided to give back the pay cuts we all took in 1968—for some of the staff—but not me. I knew, because I wrote all the payroll checks, although they brought in a woman to learn a new-fangled computer system that was supposed to streamline accounting operations.

I went to the office manager for Robert Lurie, the club's owner, to plead my case, asking that my pay also be brought back to its pre-Oakland-coming-to-town level.

His answer was simple. "Sorry, Fred, but we can't do that right now."

After 18 years with the San Francisco Giants, following countless weekends and untold hours of service, it all came down to that. I recalled how I felt back at Buffalo Solvents and Chemicals, when my promised raise wasn't given to me after ten years of hard work—and how I quit that company. It all came down to respect.

Right there, I took a breath and stated, "Well, I have to give you my two months' notice then."

Two weeks later, Robert Lurie found out and told his manager to return my pay to its original salary. He did—but it was too late for me. I was already committed to moving on.

* * *

There was a sense of uncertainty about my predicament that I always worked hard to avoid. Everything about my world was orderly and well-planned out—from the times and places I took my dogs for walks, the nightclubs I occasionally visited, to my parking spot at Candlestick Park.

I called up my brother Andy who still lived in San Diego. "So, Andy, how would you like your 55-year-old brother as your neighbor?"

I looked down at my puppies, both staring up at me. "What do you think, boys? Want to move to San Diego?"

They danced around my feet. I picked up a tennis ball and tossed it across the room with both of them diving under the sofa to retrieve it and bring it back to me.

"But, Fred, what about your job?"

"I quit." I let my words sink in before I asked, "Can your realtor find me a place?"

"Sure, Fred, sure. You know how much you like it here every time you visit. You've got two nieces who like you a lot."

"And I really like your family too."

"There's plenty of jobs for bookkeepers here—and I'd like having you around."

So, every weekend for the next month, I flew down to San Diego until I found a place. The realtor who got me my house in San Francisco six years before, put it on the market. I originally paid $30,000 for that first home and ended up selling it for $70,000 five years later—more than enough to get me situated in San Diego and start a new life. (On a trip to San Francisco in 2006, I checked on my old home and found it recently sold for $900,000!).

I drove south on I-5 following the United Van Lines filled with all my furniture. My VW Bug carried my two dogs, a big ceramic donkey I used as a garden gnome, and as many fuchsias

174

as I could fit in. The city looked different to me this time because it would be my new home. Memories of the first time I came to San Diego came back to me.

That was January 1946, right after my time in the Navy in the Pacific during WWII. Then there were all the trips I took to visit my brother and his family every year during the holidays since I moved to San Francisco 18 years before.

A world of new adventures awaited me, Brandy, and Angus.

Anchors aweigh!

20

My older brother, Andy, Jr., worked for Solar Turbines in San Diego as a corporate lawyer and had a good friend who was a real estate agent. With the $40,000 in my pocket I cleared from the sale of my house in San Francisco, it didn't take me long to find a place during weekend jaunts to San Diego. I put $20,000 down on a $50,000 home on Orchard Avenue near the far south side of Ocean Beach, in an area called Point Loma Highlands. I still live in the same home, and the last time I checked, it was worth $900,000!

Lots of work waited for me in this house with its worn thick blue shag carpet and old fixtures. Even Brandy and Angus couldn't stand the smell of our new home. After I had all the carpet ripped out, the paint-stained wood floors were next. Sanding, staining, sealing—finally, it was clean and neat. I added a kitchen garden window to look out over my back yard and it brought in lots of additional light. Then it felt like home.

In addition to my change in location from San Francisco to San Diego, change was happening everywhere in 1976, my 55th year. In May, I contracted a bladder and prostate infection.

Seems my prostate was too big. The first operation, since my tonsils were taken out when I was seven, took place at Mercy Hospital and it went smoothly. However, this marked the beginning of a series of operations I'd go through over the next three-plus decades.

The second home I owned and currently live in.

America held July 4th bicentennial celebrations with parades and flags, and tall ships, especially in my new military town with its strong Navy and Marine connections. On the same day, halfway around the world in a place called Entebbe, Israeli commandos rescued 103 Air France passengers from pro-Palestinian hijackers. A month later, the world named a new disease because it killed 29 American Legionnaires following their convention in Philadelphia. In September, the San Francisco Giants finished fourth and I wished them luck. Then in November, a peanut farmer from Georgia was elected the

39th President of the United States. That's what was happening in the world from my new home in San Diego.

* * *

I took the opportunity to go to New York for a quick vacation—to take in some Broadways and visit with my brother John. We saw *The Ritz*, about a Men's bath house; *Grand Hotel*, where we had 4th^{thth}-row orchestra seats; and, *Sugar Babies*, with Mickey Rooney and Ann Miller, seated in the left section of the orchestra. When we came back from intermission, a man was sitting in our seats. He excused himself and got up. He was one of the actors and was there to open the second act. He was a "pitch" man!

* * *

I wasn't used to being unemployed, so I was more than ready when I landed a job six months into my San Diego adventure. I answered an ad in the *San Diego Union* for an office manager and bookkeeper at the New Frontier Trading Corporation. Just from the name, my mind conjured up all kinds of different products the company might be trading— antiquities, paintings or coins, maybe even rare fabrics or jewels. I was in for an unpleasant surprise.

For my interview, I brought along a hand-written letter of recommendation from Horace Stoneham, the owner of the Giants (as you'd expect, I kept the letter), and one from the

Buffalo Solvent and Chemical Company. My eighteen years with the reputable Giants went a long way to impress the owner.

My new work place ended up being just one small office with two facing desks. My boss, Mr. José Kahn, a German Jew from Chile, was a small older man with huge ears. He never smiled and talked less. You won't believe what the company did. Instead of something exotic, they made lead weights, 20 and 50-pound ingots in a factory over the border in Tijuana, Mexico. Ballast, window sashes, dumbwaiters, lots of things you'd never guess lead would be used for.

I'd meet with Mr. Kahn in the office each morning for a few minutes—a few short words, then he was off to the factory across the border in Tijuana. I spent my days alone, handling the phone, taking care of all the paperwork—invoices, the books, collections, and correspondence.

During lunch, I drove my VW Bug 2.8 miles to my home to see Brandy and Angus, and to grab a bite to eat—a tuna fish sandwich, an apple, maybe a few cookies. I tossed tennis balls to my boys in the back yard for a while, gave them a few treats—and then it was back to the office. Day after day, the same routine—and I liked it.

Two months into my new job, that first Christmas in 1976, told me everything I needed to know about the company I would stay with for 21 years. Mr. Kahn gave me and his best customers FFC's. You can't guess what that was? They were "Freakin' Fruit Cakes!" I never understood how congealed pieces of petrified fruit-like "nuggets" encased in some kind of dark, sweet cake could be considered worthy of a bonus or a gift.

I always gave mine to my sister-in-law and she loved them. I was tempted to keep one for a year just to see if it was capable of getting mold, or maybe use it as a doorstop. It was then I realized how lucky I was back at the Buffalo Solvent and Chemical Company in the 1950's—I used to scoff at their $50 yearly bonus, plus two quarts of anti-freeze.

Speaking of company bonuses, I forgot to mention that the San Francisco Giants gave their employees Christmas gifts, the same favors they handed out to season ticket holders. One year they created custom playing cards imprinted with their logo and boxed them in classy soft black leather cases. I was able to get my hands on twenty of them and they came in handy.

I remembered Gladys Martin, a long-time friend from Albany and came up with a fun idea. She was in charge of a secretarial pool of ladies who worked for New York State's Freeway Authority. I neatly wrapped each leather case in holiday paper with ribbons and bows, then sent them to her. When I took a trip to New York City, I stopped to see her and her staff, and boy, I was a hit.

Gladys mentioned how she'd like to maybe come out to California sometime for a visit. I gave her my standard answer, "Sure. Any time would be fine."

Well, eight months after I moved into my new home in San Diego, any time happened. I thought Gladys would stay for a week, but it turned into a two-month vacation. Since I had a spare room with two twin beds, she settled in fine. What did we do? I drove her everywhere in my VW—beaches, La Jolla, Del Mar, Coronado, even taking her to visit my niece in Murietta, up past Temecula.

We had some nice times, falling into a good rhythm during weekdays. When I'd come home from work for lunch, she'd have a meal waiting for me. Just to be clear about this, we were just friends, no canoodling or hanky-panky going on—okay?

* * *

During my first year at work, Mr. Kahn, my boss, took me to his factory in Tijuana. Crossing the border was like entering another world—street vendors and crippled people coming up to his car, all with their hands out. The *factory* ended up being an open building with a furnace situated in the middle of a huge dirt lot. Rusting piles of scrap metal and batteries littered the ground—Mexican workers grabbing the junk and tossing it into the furnace. It reeked.

He bought me lunch at a small restaurant on the way back toward the border crossing, the only time he ever did. I don't eat tacos or spicy foods, so I had a torta—a ham and cheese sandwich with some bland cheese and strange mayonnaise.

* * *

To trim my ever-thinning hair, I found a barber in Point Loma on Rosecrans at Dickens, not far from my home. Louis Paulerio and his younger brother, Virgil, immigrated to the

United States from Portugal when they were teenagers. What fun and lively men. They spoke to the waiting Portuguese customers while they cut my hair—a large group of them left over from the tuna fishing fleets from years past. Over 39 years, I got to see their shop entertainment evolve from just a radio, to a small black and white TV, then to a high-definition color flat screen with more channels than you could imagine.

I heard that famous singer Frankie Laine got up early every Tuesday morning to be first in line to have his hair trimmed and get a shave. With iconic songs like *Mule Train*, the theme from the TV show *Rawhide*, and the hit *Lucky Old Sun*—he was a legend. Frankie stood in front of the red-white-and-blue turning barber pole reading a newspaper. I beat him there once and he was none too happy, but we started talking and ended up having a very nice chat. Later I learned he wore a toupee because he was so bald—that's when I figured he only went in for a trim and a shave.

Sad thing about the Pauliero's—in May 2015, their landlord cancelled their lease. After 55 years in business, and nearly four decades cutting my hair, they closed their doors. No more GQ or Esquire magazines, or the pungent scents of tonic and aftershave amidst the brothers' heavy-accented banter.

* * *

When I moved to San Diego in 1976, they didn't have any Broadway shows except for a few road companies and some local theater. I was so homesick for high-quality live entertainment, a few times I flew to San Francisco on either a Saturday or Sunday morning, had lunch, took in a matinee, and returned home in time to take my dogs for their last walk around the block for the day. I got to see the Russian Ballet and their incredible dancers, La Cage aux Folles (the Bird Cage), and Evita with Patti LuPone and Mandy Patinkin.

One time, Henny Youngman sat in front of me in my third-row seat orchestra seat, and as we were walking up the aisle after the show I just had to whisper to him, "Take my wife, please," his famous comedy line. He turned around and thanked me.

* * *

Because I always looked fit, I've been asked many times by friends and acquaintances—"What did you do for exercise, Fred?"

Well, I walked my dogs around the block—walked to the beach, around town. Not hiking—walking. Lots and lots of walking. I wore out plenty of shoes along the way.

* * *

On a Monday morning in January 1979, 16-year-old Brenda Spencer looked out the window from her home over at the Grover Cleveland Elementary School in San Diego. She raised a .22 rifle and began shooting. By the time she finished, the principal and the custodian were dead, and nine children injured. She later told police, "I just don't like Mondays."

That was be the first school shooting in San Diego, and would be the only one committed by a girl. It hit me hard that day, knowing we were living in a new sad, sad, world, where people killed for no other reason than the day of the week.

21

While I was busy living my life, my parents were living theirs. In 1959, a year after I moved to San Francisco, Dad retired from The Great Atlantic & Pacific Tea Company—you know it as the A&P. They moved from Kenmore (right outside of Buffalo) to Boca Raton, Florida. That same year, Alaska and Hawaii were admitted to the Union, Barbie Doll made her debut, gas was 25 cents a gallon, and you could watch Oscar Winner Charleton Heston race a chariot at a movie theater for only a dollar.

My dad, Andrew Hillhouse, Sr., spent 45 years with the A&P and received many promotions along the way, each one causing us to move to yet another town across the northeast. I think he was also ready to retire because their house in Kenmore felt so empty with their four children scattered across the country. Andy Jr., my only sibling to marry and have children, lived in San Diego where he worked as a corporate lawyer for Solar Energy. John, nine years younger than me, worked for the A&P in New York City. And my sister Nancy, 11 years younger than me, was employed by the Atomic Energy Commission in Los Angeles.

So started the Hillhouse children's bi-yearly pilgrimages to Florida, alternating with our parents coming out to visit us in California, but rarely would all six of us gather at the same time. We fell into a nice pattern of coast-to-coast travel that allowed me to get the latest news, as only my mother could convey it, about my siblings.

* * *

I forgot to mention, but shortly after my mother passed in late 1970, Dad took up with Grace, a woman they both knew who lived across the street from them in Boca. She was your typical little old lady. I knew he would never want to live alone, the way he and Mother had their morning, evening, and weekend routines. With us four children scattered all over the country, it made sense. He liked to play golf, she liked to watch him—a perfect match. They moved in together and started up a life. During the next nine years, I never visited them and they never made it out to see me.

I kept in touch with Dad with an occasional letter or card, but usually by phone. "How's your golf game, Dad?"

"Fine, Fred. Just fine. Shot an eight-two and picked up eight bucks from Willard and Joe, you remember them."

"Yeah." Not that I was interested, but I knew he liked it, so I asked, "How's Grace?"

For the next ten minutes, he went on about how she decorated something, he took her somewhere, or she cooked him a fabulous meal. He was happy. That's all that mattered.

"Well," I always said, my cue to him that our chat had come to an end. "Talk to you soon, Dad."

"Take care, Fred."

That was that.

* * *

During my annual visit to see my father in 1977, I had an impulse that I acted on—nothing huge, but fun. Before I left for the airport to return to San Diego, I went to the beach and dipped my toes in the Atlantic Ocean. After touching down in San Diego, my first stop was Ocean Beach, where I dipped my toes in the Pacific Ocean. Ahh!

That's the Atlantic on the left and the Pacific on the right

* * *

On May 12, 1979, my niece Susan Hillhouse married Guy Beach. The wedding took place at the Presbyterian Church in Point Loma about one mile from my house.

Susan Hillhouse and Guy Beach Wedding

* * *

Later in 1979, three years after I moved to San Diego, I got a call from my brother Andy. "You better get to Boca quick," he ended our conversation.

Dad had been struck down by a cerebral hemorrhage. I hopped the first flight from San Diego to Boca, my heart pounding in my chest the entire trip—memories flooding my eyes as I looked out the window at the odd-shaped patches of topography below me. Unending acres and miles of crops, forests, prairies, mountains, and 225 million Americans who would never know Dad's name, or that he was dying.

They served some kind of beef stroganoff on top of a lukewarm block of egg noodles that I barely touched, then I partially watched *Heaven Can Wait,* the inflight movie. After that, I put on my airline headset and tried to sleep, but Sly and the Family Stone's hit song, *We are Family* kept me awake. How ironic it was with the last origins of my family gone.

I waited with my brothers and sister—Andy Jr., John, and Nancy—in the hospital lounge. Hard plastic orange chairs, wrinkled copies of old Time Magazine issues, a gray pay phone in the corner of the room, and harsh overhead fluorescent lights kept the mood even more glum. We didn't say much—we weren't that kind of family.

Eventually, the doctor came out, his forehead wrinkled with concern. We stood. "It looks like your father is about to pass. Would any of you like to be with him—to say goodbye?"

We looked to each other without response. John stepped forward. "I do."

He left the waiting room and returned half an hour later. "He's gone," he stated simply, the weight and finality of his words stinging my eyes.

Nancy began to cry. Andy and I just looked at each other and slowly shook our heads.

His death certificate, I have my mother's as well, stated that he died of cardiovascular disease. At his memorial service three days later, I made sure that the same pastor who conducted my mother's ceremony referred to him as Andy, not Mr. Hillhouse. That was nice.

In the year that President Jimmy Carter got attacked by a swamp rabbit, a gay rights march was held in Washington, D.C., and McDonald's introduced their "Happy Meal," Dad was cremated, just like my mother. I don't remember whatever happened to the ashes.

* * *

When it came time for Dad's estate to be settled a week later, there was little left, the last nine years of his life spent enjoying time with his companion, Grace. My oldest brother, Andy Jr., the executor of our Dad's estate, suggested we give Grace a full share in the final disbursement. John and Nancy nodded along with me.

It's funny the things we find out about loved ones after they're gone. In going through his things, we discovered a sleeve of five golf balls—each with the date, course, and hole number where he aced holes-in-one. My brother Andy Jr. took those, and rightly so, the jock of my siblings growing up. John, always the reader in the family, selected a few of his books. Nancy had already gone through my mother's stuff nine years before, but she took the plaid scarf Dad used to wear when he played golf on chilly mornings. There were Dad's discharge papers from WWI—I got them being the military man with the most service in our family.

The morning before I left to catch my flight back to San Diego, we went to the bank where Andy Jr. zeroed out all the accounts and handed each of us a $17,000 cashier's check.

Looking out the window of the plane, I thought of the ways I'd spend my inheritance. Andy told me about an investment opportunity in an apartment building in Texas and I joined in. It gave me write-offs for four years, which I didn't really need.

* * *

With our parents gone, us four siblings kept in touch, usually by phone, sometimes a letter or a birthday card. Nancy worked for the Atomic Energy Commission in Los Angeles, and then moved with them to Los Alamos, New Mexico. John switched jobs, going from A&P corporate management to business manager at the Marble Collegiate Church in Manhattan. Norman Vincent Peale preached there at the time, most famous for his book, *The Power of Positive Thinking*.

I spoke to Andy Jr. almost weekly because he lived in town. Of course, I attended all of his family's activities. Birthdays, graduations, Fourth of July, Thanksgiving, and Christmas. I became "Uncle Fred" to his two daughters, my nieces, Susan and Sara—and found myself enjoying the role of the doting uncle who lived nearby.

I never thought it unusual, but Andy Jr. was the only sibling of us four to marry and have children. I've heard stories of people who had such bad childhoods, horrible parents who mistreated them, so horrible that the children couldn't imagine marriage and families. That wasn't us.

* * *

191

All of my seven pets died at 13 years old, except for Brandy II—he lasted 17 years. The first to go was Brandy in 1980, my Boston Terrier, and first pet. Every time he lost a baby tooth, he'd drop them on the floor by my feet—like I was the tooth fairy.

Boy, did Brandy loved to pose! There were probably more photos taken with him and the San Francisco Giants office staff than there were with them and famous baseball players.

It was kidney disease that finally took him. I'm not ashamed to admit I shed many tears when I took him to the vet and had him put to sleep. Brandy's ashes, 11 teeth, water bowl, and pictures rest on a shelf in my bedroom now with memorabilia from all my pets who are gone.

* * *

1980 was also a challenging year at work. My boss had me rent a storage room by our parking lot to keep some stock, lead weights—which I delivered to customers sometimes in my VW Bug. Trucks would come from our four-acre Tijuana plant,

Metales y Derivados, and I would unload 7,000 pounds of lead weights. My hips and knees felt it.

Since he detested talking, I wrote a letter to Mr. Kahn asking for a raise. I added a final statement. "You treat me like a Mexican peon."

He never responded. That and the yearly fruitcake set the tone for the 21 years I worked for him—always unsaid words providing the friction that defined our relationship. How it ended, in 1997 when I was 76 years old, was even sadder than how it began. He got his due though, but I'll get to that later.

* * *

I took one of my life's rare vacations, calling up American Airlines and seeing if they could recommend something for me. So, I took a trip to Mexico City where I stayed at the Hilton Hotel, and then on to Acapulco at the Hilton there as well. My meager French lessons in high school didn't help much, but most of the waiters and bartenders spoke English, so I got along just fine. Across the street from the hotel was a popular bar I chose as my hang out for the week. There was a Hollywood convention going on, which meant I got to see some stars.

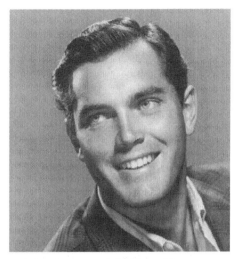

The first night I spotted Jeffrey Hunter two seats down from me—kissing his friend. Later, he danced with a heavy-set woman adorned in jewels. I suspected she was the wife of a Hollywood mogul.

* * *

Some things we embrace about our heritage. For me it's the Hillhouse name and its place in American history. William Bradford, a 10th-generation-removed relative from the Mayflower, and noted historian of the early Plymouth Plantation, brings me a lot of pride. In 1980, after gathering reams of paperwork, much of it copied from old bibles and birth certificates dating back to the 1600s, and submitting it for approval, I was accepted into The Mayflower Society. I framed the certificate. Since then, I've paid my yearly dues and still enjoy receiving their newsletters. I've never been to one of their meetings because they're usually held somewhere on the East Coast.

I didn't inherit Dad's athleticism, but I did get my mother's arthritis. She used to knit to keep her hands nimble to fight it off in her later years. Afghans, sweaters for her two granddaughters, sometimes a wool cap. After she passed away in 1970, we found a dresser filled with sweaters she knitted, every color imaginable, some with rhinestones and gems embedded in them. They were small, just like her. I brought them back with me to San Francisco and a friend from San Diego ended up getting them.

Also in 1980, my joints began to ache. Three years later would mark the first of many "procedures" I would undergo for my hips and right knee, keeping my orthopedic doctor in new Mercedes' for years to come. The physical decline of one Fred Hillhouse began at 59 years old, and there was nothing I could do to stop it.

Oh well, life goes on. It has for 95 years so far.

22

Nineteen-eighty-one was a sobering year for me in many ways. It started with 52 American hostages being released by Iran the day Reagan took office in January, Disneyland had its first homicide, Mohammed Ali retired—and I quit drinking.

You might think this odd, I sure do, but I don't have any record of the actual day I stopped—no receipts to file, no notes to sort, no doctor's statement or records to catalog.

I have very few regrets in my life. One is that I didn't stop drinking sooner. At 60-years-old, with over 40 years of heavy weekend drinking, I quit—cold turkey. When I look back at the amount of money I spent on drinking, I regret that even more than the hangovers. As you can imagine, I tallied up the cost of my drinking over 40 years—I was stunned—$132,617!

It might have helped that my young brother, John, called me, his voice the happiest I'd heard in years. "Fred, you know how I've been a heavy drinker."

"Yeah, John, you sure know how to tie one on."

"Well, I realized that alcohol was controlling my life, so many of my decisions centered around my next drink."

His words floated in the air, waiting for me. "So, John?"

"Well, I joined Alcoholics Anonymous in 1972."

"I heard of them."

"I've already been to lots of meetings, and I'm telling you, I think it's the only way for me to stop."

"I'm glad for you, John." I went over and fiddled with a window shade, working to pull it down all the way—but it kept on rolling up and wouldn't catch.

"The meetings are filled with people, just like you and me, you know, professionals, who are trying to quit drinking and drugs. It might be good for you too."

"That's wonderful for you, John." I took a deep breath, trying to the find the right words to tell him I didn't need a crutch like that, a room full of people who recited pledges, sponsors calling you day and night, handing out little coins like they were good conduct medals from kindergarten. I'd met more than a handful of "former" AA members at bars I frequented—that's how I knew about their program, and how well it worked. "I'll be fine, really."

"I'm just saying, Fred—"

I cut him off. "I got it, John. Thanks for the call and good luck with your drinking, or should I say, getting on the wagon."

*   *   *

We watched our parents drink and followed their lead. Highballs and cocktails when they went out on the town every Friday night to the Park Lane Hotel for dinner when they lived in Buffalo. Sherry and jugs of wine around the house when we were kids—those were staples in our lives. They were happy drinkers, not the kind of parents who would raise their voices, or scream obscenities, or beat their children. We noticed.

I always enjoyed a good time drinking in bars and clubs, listening to live music, slowly draining a cold beer, then buying performers drinks and chatting them up. In 1936, when I was 15 years old, I snuck into Utica bars and order beers. At a slender 160 pounds, but 6'2", I was never asked for my identification—and they didn't care much about that in 1937.

I didn't drink while I was in Boston where I went to accounting college when I was 19. For me, being away from home was all about going to live theater, Vaudeville shows, and movies. Besides, drinking cost too much on my limited student budget.

When I came back home to Utica, I took to lounging around and going out with my friends to dance and drink. After incessant urging from Dad, I got a job, then came my notice from the draft to join the Army for WWII. Instead, I joined the Navy. I couldn't see it at the time, but my drinking and my attitude about not studying and simply enjoying myself, played a big part in everything that followed in my life.

I picked up my drinking ways right after my three-and-a-half years in the Navy when I moved to New York City. The clubs there stayed open to four in the morning, beers were fifty cents each, and the cover charge at the nicer places was $1.25— that was a lot since I made only $1.00 an hour with Chase National.

After doormen got to know me, I walked right past the patrons waiting in line. A smile and a tip to the hat check girl when I dropped off my coat, and then I took up residence at the corner of the bar for the night.

I already told you this, but after my two years in The City, I moved in with my parents in their new home in Kenmore, just outside of Buffalo. To get a nice "edge" going and a start on a Friday or Saturday evening, and to save a few bucks, I made myself vodka martinis or vodka on the rocks at home before I'd head out to a club. For those ten years in Buffalo, I fell into the same weekend pattern of enjoying life. Nothing as a bookkeeper for Buffalo Solvents and Chemicals challenged me much, so that was how I spent my weekends—beers, live entertainment—good times.

Throughout all my years at clubs and bars, I never drank with anyone from work. My drinking buddies were from my neighborhood or friends I met at bars. Sometimes I'd head over to a neighbor's house for an impromptu party, and someone would bring a big jug of wine, mostly in San Francisco. When we drained it, the seeds at the bottom would stain our teeth— but we didn't care.

I did less weekend drinking during my 18 years in San Francisco, the Giants keeping me so busy when they weren't on the road. I also had the responsibilities of my house and my dogs. One time, I downed 10 beers in a San Francisco bar. I stumbled out the door at closing and weaved my way to my car, barely getting my key in the ignition. I don't remember driving the two miles home up Market Street. After that, I told myself to slow down—five beers maximum, not ten!

I realize now that if I didn't drink like I did, my life could have gone in a completely different direction. Maybe a college diploma would have been handed to me. Maybe I would have landed better jobs, found a sweetheart to marry, and started a family.

But life's not about "maybe's."

* * *

One of my last drinking adventures was on huge RV scooting around San Diego. A friend of a friend of mine owned a huge 65-footer—that was our ride. Zane Vaughn invited me to come along as her date for the night, and we joined six other couples. What a hoot. We started out in Loma Square where we parked our cars at Midway and Rosecrans. We stopped here and there for cocktails and ended up at the Town and Country Hotel in Mission Valley for dinner, more drinks, and dancing. I did lots of both that night.

* * *

A wonderful joy came into my life in June 1981—Brandon Beach, my great-nephew, and son of Susan (my niece who lives in Murrieta) and Guy Beach. I felt like a grandpa in many ways and found myself wanting to dote on him. His tragic end 27 years later is something that still haunts me.

I sobered up more in 1981 when I discovered my finances were in trouble because of my credit cards. That was extra embarrassing because I was a bookkeeper and should have known better. With six credit cards, mostly maxed out, I was stuck making minimum payments each month. The habit of borrowing from one with an increasing credit limit to pay off others finally caught up to me.

Luckily, I found a pro bono attorney to help me out and he negotiated five of the credit cards down to almost nothing. However, a bounty hunter from Chase came after me for the $10,000 I owed them. After a few months of his never-ending phone calls and threatening letters, I cut a deal for $5,000, but don't remember how I came up with the money to pay them off. I know, that's not like me.

Since then, I've never had any trouble with credit cards, always living within my meager means. By the age of 60, I'd already spent five years at the New Frontier Trading Company, and didn't believe I could land another job that paid any better. Mr. Kahn, my angry little boss knew that too—that's why he kept on giving me more work to do and seldom any raise.

The year I quit drinking, in 1981, ended with the first American test-tube baby being born in Virginia, and CNN debuting on December 31st. I was more than glad the year was over, filled with the sobering after-effects of no more bars, no more drinking, no more friends who drank, and no more credit card debt.

1982 had to be better.

23

There was a lot going on in 1982, but not for me. I was adjusting to life without alcohol, no bar buddies, and no free-spending with credit cards—but I did attack my yard with renewed vigor and I got to know my neighbors with the extra time on my hands.

John Belushi died in March, the British fought Argentina over the Falkland Islands in April, Princess Grace died when her car plunged over a cliff in September, *Cats* opened on Broadway in October, and Michael Jackson released *Thriller* in November. Like I said, a lot happening that year, but not for me.

I kept myself busy at the New Frontier Trading Company, doing the wishes of Mr. Kahn, the owner. I even babysat his cat at his home when he went on vacation with his family, and as always, nothing more than a few words from him every morning before he left for his plant in Tijuana.

"Did you send out the invoice to the XYZ Company?"

"Yes, Mr. Kahn."

"I'm going to the plant," he'd grumble.

That was the same drill for the next years.

* * *

The next few years were much the same—work, taking care of my pets, even adding two new ones. My niece had a friend who lived in Point Loma who just had a litter of cats. They were free, so why not add to my growing family? I named them Johnny and Nancy (after my younger brother and sister). They had pure white fur, and became my indoor cats. Before they would come into my house though, I had to de-flea them.

I went to the library to find out the best way to treat it. I took them to my back yard and set up a small bath of diluted rubbing alcohol. Dip. Comb. Dip. Comb. As the small black fleas fled for dry ground in the mess of fur, I poured more alcohol on them and combed them out. The cats twisted and

FRED HILLHOUSE

scratched my hands, but I repeated softly, "It'll be okay. You'll feel so much better when I'm finished."

* * *

I attended Mr. Kahn's son's funeral, and wore a Yamaka. Mr. Kahn didn't even thank me for attending, his yearly holiday fruitcakes probably his idea of thanks for everything.

I re-discovered my passion for live theater, attending many of the La Jolla Playhouse productions. I could afford tickets now that I had extra spending money I wasn't throwing away at bars and nightclubs.

* * *

Early in 1984, Angus, my beautiful Terrier mix dog, fell ill. I knew he felt puny when he wouldn't touch any of the four dishes of food I put on the floor for him—popcorn in one, chicken in another, wet dog food in the third, and dry dog food in the last. I sat in my bedroom chair holding him, rocking him back and forth, whispering in his ears everything I felt about him, recalling so many memories over the past 13 years. Angus' breath got shallow, he gulped for air, and then his head flopped to the side. I held him for probably an hour.

In the year when Mondale and Ferraro challenged Reagan for the presidency, the Padres lost to Detroit in the World Series, and when Union Carbide killed 2,000 and injured 150,000 more in India—my beloved Angus was cremated. His ashes rest in a small spruce box next to Brandy's on a shelf in my room. I never cried so much in my life, deep sobs taking hold of me at the most unexpected moments.

Understanding my deep loss, my brother Andy showed up at my home a few weeks later with a puppy I named Brandy II. It didn't take long, though, before his young puppy ways got the best of me. I had just re-upholstered my living room couch at a cost of $1,000—a lot of money in 1984. I came home from work for my normal lunch and found one whole arm of my couch thoroughly chewed up.

I was never so mad in my life. I got a hold of him, held him in front of my destroyed couch and spanked him again and again. "Bad boy. You're such a bad boy," I repeated.

He whimpered and shook, and when I set him down, he ran into the next room and hid under the bed. To this day, I've never felt so bad about anything I've done. It is one of the few regrets I carry in my heart.

* * *

On cool Point Loma mornings, usually in the winter, my joints began to ache—both hips and my right knee. I saw an orthopedic doctor in 1988 and his diagnosis was simple.

"Arthritis, Mr. Hillhouse. Did you play a lot of sports when you were young?"

"No."

"Is there a history of arthritis in your family?"

"My mother—her hands a little."

"Well, at your age," he glanced down at my medical file, "at 67 years old, I'd expect something to start slowing you down." He grabbed a pen off his desk and picked up a pad. "I'm writing you a prescription for some mild pain relievers. Let's keep an eye on this every year when you come see me for a check-up."

He handed me the slip and I left his office, certain I was getting slower and older.

* * *

While my joints ached, I added to my menagerie that year with two more kittens, Mandy and Sandy. My next door neighbor was into rebuilding old cars and had a growing collection of rusting car parts resting against the faded brown wooden fence that separated our yards. I heard some small "mews" coming from his property while I pulled weeds in my garden. I went over and found a malnourished street cat with four baby kittens.

I lured her over to my yard with some food and the kittens followed. I built a small enclosure for them as she fattened up and the kittens' health improved. I checked on them at least three times a day—in the morning, when I came home for lunch, and just before it got dark. One day, the mother didn't come home, so I took the kittens to the vet, then brought Mandy and Sandy back to my home where they officially joined my family, now grown to Brandy II and four cats. What a wonderful Christmas we had in 1988.

In late January, 1989, the San Francisco 49ers won the Super Bowl. Yes, I know, I hadn't lived there for the past 13

years, but I still felt very connected to the city with friends I'd write or call, or sometimes visit.

My second grand-nephew, William, was born in 1989 to my niece Sara who lived in France. My doting of another young relative doubled that special day.

In October of the same year, I drove to San Francisco for a week's stay, the Littlefield's putting me up. We were playing cards when a 6.9 earthquake struck, just before the start of the third game of the World Series between Oakland and San Francisco. We looked at each other in alarm, got up quickly and stood around the kitchen entry—doorways supposed to be the safest place.

When the shaking stopped, I blurted out, "That was a strong one."

"Turn on the TV," someone said.

We watched as news stations began to show us the devastation. When they tallied everything up a few days later, 26 people were dead and over 100,000 buildings were damaged. I had tickets for several theater shows but they were all canceled, so I drove home early.

* * *

The rhythm and pattern of my life continued much the same until the birth of another grand-nephew, Henry, in 1990 to Sara (in France)—adding to my Christmas card list.

Nothing much to report until Saturday morning, December 14, 1991, I walked out of my home to run some errands in my first and only car, my VW Bug—but it was gone. Stolen. I felt violated. Nothing bad like that had ever happened to me. A month before, a good Samaritan left a note on my windshield with a warning. I still have the note. I showed it to the police.

Dear Sir –

I overheard some students talk about taking your beautiful car. I want to warn you about putting your bug in a safe place so it won't get stolen.

You might wonder who I am, but I'm just a person that has a bug and appreciates the originality of yours.

Please take care of your car.

Yours truly,

Someone who cares

My precious VW wasn't worth much, and my insurance paid out very little—but it was enough to buy an old blue Dodge Colt from a neighbor. It ran alright with a manual transmission, just like my Bug, but it wasn't a Bug.

The house grew quiet with just Brandy II and me, usually cuddled up on the couch at night watching TV together. I caught him wandering around the house looking for Nancy and Johnny, then coming back and sitting in front of me, his sad eyes asking where his friends had gone.

I knew just how he felt.

24

In the year Audrey Hepburn died, the first humans were cloned, and 72 Branch Dividians burned to death after a 51-day standoff with the FBI in Texas, my right hip got replaced—the pain from my arthritis becoming just too much. 1993 was a difficult year in so many respects—filled with recovery, getting used to walking again, and working from home on Mr. Khan's books for several months. He was none too happy I wasn't in the office, obviously missing our boisterous morning conversations which amounted to him grunting he was going to the factory.

Brandy II and my four cats kept me company through all of it. My brother Andy and his daughters visited as well. I reached out to Point Loma Nazarene University to find a trustworthy student who could drive me to appointments and errands. That began a long-term relationship between me, and the university, and a lot of incredible young people—relationships that remain to this day.

If you're not familiar with PLNU, their campus is situated five minutes from my home on the north side of the peninsula that juts out into the vast blue Pacific. Over 3,000 clean-cut students—no tattoos or piercings, no smoking, drugs or alcohol—occupy the most beautiful college campus in America. Each of the 21 students who helped me over the years have been of tremendous character and attitude. It made me feel good to know that as they were helping me, the pay I gave them also made their education more affordable. I stay in touch with a handful of them by phone and then yearly with my Christmas cards.

* * *

In 1995, I added another grand-nephew to my life with the birth of Joseph, again to Sara in France, making it four grand-nephews—Brandon, William, Henry, and Joseph.

The following year rolled by and I became so used to my new painless right hip, that the pain in my left one really stood out. So, I had surgery on it in February 1996. During my recovery at home, Mr. Kahn brought me his books to manage, dumping them on my front doorstep unceremoniously with a note that simply stated, 'Here they are.'

When I wasn't calling up Mr. Kahn's customers about overdue invoices, I spent much of my spare time researching and gathering the paperwork needed to join The Mayflower Society. Since I was a tenth-generation-removed descendant of William Bradford, the Pilgrim's first governor, I felt it was finally time to get this done or forget about it.

Recovery of my left hip went so well, that in November 1996, I had my right knee replaced, just after the Clinton/Gore ticket defeated Dole/Kemp to remain in office for a second term. With all the metal in me, my friends began calling me the bionic man—and I got a kick out of that.

The year ended with some sadness as I recalled the deaths of Ella Fitzgerald, Gene Kelly, and George Burns. Ella was special to me because she sang at my high school's Phi Delta Sigma, Alpha Chapter, fraternity Christmas party in 1939. Dark-haired, bright-eyed, and sweet-smiling Margarite Cullen danced with me that entire evening, in fact, all through high school—but five years later she broke my heart.

* * *

Early in 1996, my first two cats, Johnny and Nancy both got sick. I took them to the vet.

After a round of expensive tests, Dr. Rose told me, "Feline leukemia. It's fairly common, Mr. Hillhouse."

"What are my options?" I asked, stroking my white cats, trying to keep them calm.

"You might get a few more years out of them, maybe reach 15, if I treat them—but the cost might be prohibitive, especially with two cats."

They were suffering. I didn't have $2,500, so I had them put to sleep and then cremated. Their ashes joined Brandy's and Angus' on the shelf in my room, the loss of four of my darling pets mounting.

* * *

On an ordinary day in February 1997, as usual, Mr. Kahn swung by to pick up the books, the letters and invoices I'd written, and checks to be signed. I hobbled out to the curb favoring my right knee, clutching all the paperwork under my free arm. I leaned in the passenger window and placed all the papers on the seat.

"Is that everything?" he asked, the car engine still running.

"Yes."

"Well, I guess that's it then."

That comment was out of the ordinary, too many words. So I asked, "What do mean?"

"I won't be requiring your services any longer."

"What? Are you firing me?"

"If you want put it that way, yes." He put his transmission into drive, his foot still on the brake.

"What—what about severance?"

He started to shake. "What's that?" He wouldn't make eye contact.

"I worked for you for 21 years. I fed your cat when you went on vacation. For Christ's sake, I wore a yamaka to your son's funeral. I delivered thousands of pounds of lead weights for you, using my car, and you only paid me ten cents a mile after I begged you—and never a thank you."

"I've got to go," he mumbled, and pulled away from the curb.

Son of bitch.

I yelled after him, "And I never ate your fucking fruitcakes."

* * *

I was stunned, and stood in the middle of street for a long time until a car honked at me, then I hobbled inside. I closed the door behind me and leaned up against it, a long, deep sigh escaping my lips. It hit me hard—I had no idea how I would make ends meet. Here I was, 75 years old—no one would hire an aging bionic man like me. I knew nothing about the newfangled computers people used for bookkeeping. A dinosaur. Useless.

Brandy II and my two cats came over to me, looking up, waiting for my usual kind words—but I had nothing. After a few minutes, I looked down at them. "Looks like we're in for some stormy weather," the lines from Lena Horne's song spilling out of my mouth.

I applied for unemployment the next day. That, along with my Social Security, would bring in enough to sustain me, but not much else.

I should have seen it coming, Mr. Kahn's plant cited in 1994 for its toxic waste. I felt bad about that. Here's a piece of a report about the monumental mess he left behind.

[Of the 66 documented toxic waste sites in Mexican border states, the most infamous is Tijuana's Metales y Derivados, a U.S.-owned maquiladora factory that recycled batteries imported from the U.S. The owner, José Kahn, fled across the border when the maquiladora was shut down in 1994 after community reports of health problems and repeated violations of environmental law documented by the Mexican government. Mr. Kahn left behind 23,000 tons of mixed contaminated waste, including 7,000 tons of lead slag, exposed to the elements and threatening workers and families living in the adjacent Tijuana neighborhood of Colonia Chilpancingo.]

* * *

The next year was all about adjustment, especially living on a very fixed income. At least I had my sea legs back and could get around without any pain. Not much excitement during 1998, except for the birth of James, another grand-nephew, to Sara in France—her fourth son.

The Padres made it to the World Series, but got swept by the Yankees. Clinton was impeached. Viagra was approved, and Frank Sinatra died. I saw him twice at the Sports Arena in

San Diego, once with Eydie Gorme and Steve Lawrence, and the other time with Liza Minelli. He was a lot smaller than people thought. It was a lousy year all around.

* * *

The big to-do in 1999 was all about the Y2K scare—remember, the thing about computers not programmed to handle years with more than two digits? It was explained to me like this by one of the PLNU students. 1999 in the computer world was a 99. So, when the year 2000 was to hit, the numbers would read 00. When doing calculations for 2000 compared to 1999, you'd end up with negative numbers. Experts everywhere believed all sorts of bad things would happen—from the stock market crashing, bank ATMs not working, missiles launching by themselves, and worse.

There was some good news. My neighbor, Bob Starwalt, had Padres Saturday night tickets. I found myself buying some to join him. Walking into Qualcomm Stadium and seeing the brightly lit green field, it took me back to my years with the San Francisco Giants—only this time I was a spectator.

The highlight of the year for me was that I, Frederick Sisson Hillhouse, was officially accepted into The Mayflower Society. I held the certificate in my hands and stared at it for a long time thinking, *my blood contains DNA from my distant relative, William Bradford.* I'd just seen a special report on CNN about how you could tell you everything about your past from these unique markers in your blood, even your probable physical future.

With that certificate in hand, I also joined The Governor William Bradford Compact, The Sons of the American Revolution, The National Society of Sons of the American Colonists, and The National Society Sons of Colonial New England. Each of those documents, as you can imagine, have been framed and occupy a special place on the wall in my bedroom.

The Hillhouse siblings (l to r): John, Nancy, Andy Jr., and Fred in 1999

John F. Kennedy, Jr. tragically died in 1999 and so did Joe DiMaggio. I got Joe's autograph when I lived in Buffalo at a sports night dinner, and was asked more than once for Joe's autograph, especially during my 18 years with the San

Francisco Giants, because we were both slender and six-feet, two inches tall.

Oh, the big Y2K scare? Everyone expected to wake up January 1, 2000, to find some part of the world collapsed or stopped working. But nothing happened, pretty much like where my life was headed.

25

More of the same for me in 2,000 with my garden and predictable life, except that my 16-year-old Brandy II was slowing down, just like me—but at least I had two new hips and a new right knee. Mandy and Sandy were entering their twelfth years and becoming even more lazy, if cats can. That year, mad cow disease hit Europe hard and scared a lot of Americans, and the movie *Gladiator* came out. Then I heard how Richard Hatch, a chubby, naked, gay man, won a million dollars the first *Survivor* on TV with 51 million people watching the finale.

* * *

In February 2001, Brandy II began to wheeze and cough. Mandy and Sandy didn't seem to be doing much better, so a family outing to the vet was needed. Four weeks later, my last three pets were cremated—and just like that, I lost all my family. I'd say more, but that month was the hardest I'd gone through in years. I would have gladly traded all the pain from my surgeries for another year with my kids. Their ashes joined my other four pets on a shelf in my bedroom, accompanied by my favorite pictures of them, a few of their toys, teeth, and other mementos.

The quiet in my home only added to my sadness. How odd it was to see nothing out of place, no life in my house except for me—and not to be able to play with them again.

That was the first year I designed and sent out Christmas cards. My list of addressees was fairly simple—family and friends from San Diego to San Francisco and back to Buffalo, New Mexico for my sister, and down to Florida for my brother John.

It was a long, quiet year with only the sounds from my TV to keep me company.

God, I missed my pets.

* * *

At 80, I decided my advancing years didn't mesh too well with me taking on new pets, so that was that. Fumbling around in the garden was what I found myself doing, and then a few days every week, I had a PLNU student take me on errands. I had my pension from the Navy, my Social Security, Medicare, and no car expenses—so I was okay financially.

Eliza, my first grand-niece was born in 2002, to Sara and Francois in France—giving her five children and a total of six grand-nephews/niece to dote on. Through the years, I loved following their lives and what they were up to.

In 2002, my sister Nancy was diagnosed with lung cancer. I couldn't help but wonder if her years with the Atomic Power Commission in Los Angeles and then in Los Alamos infected her—but it was her heavy smoking that was at fault. We stayed in touch while she underwent treatment and remarked about the heroes of our youth who passed away that year—Rosemary Clooney, Peggy Lee, Billy Wilder, and Ted Williams.

* * *

What another sad year 2003 was. The Space Shuttle Columbia exploded in February, scattering debris and seven astronauts over parts of Louisiana and Texas. In March, the US invaded Iraq, searching for weapons of mass destruction—which they never found. And like it always seems to happen in threes in the entertainment world, in June, Gregory Peck, Bob Hope, and Katherine Hepburn died.

I got the call from Andy and John on Sunday, August 24, that my sister Nancy passed away. Due to a bout I was having with a bladder infection, I wasn't able to travel to Los Alamos, NM, for the funeral. That weighed on me hard the rest of the year.

They couldn't stay in her home because it smelled so bad from her incessant cigarette smoking. Since Nancy didn't have any children, Guy, my niece Susan's husband, and John stayed back to clear up her things, selling her home, closing out bank accounts and such. They brought all her paperwork back to me so I could make her final payments.

We shared in her estate which was disbursed in early 2004, each of us getting around $70,000. First on my list was a new roof, new windows and sliding doors, took down two aging pepper trees from the front yard and filled in the area with paving stones, replaced my concrete patio in the back, and a new kitchen for my aging home. Not a day goes by when I walk into my kitchen that I don't think of Nancy.

During that summer, I took my PLNU caregiver, Andrew Edmonds, with me on an East coast trip—to see family and take in some entertainment. Two days in Utica renewed old acquaintances I'd kept in touch with mostly through letters and Christmas cards. Then it was on to New York City for a week where we took in five shows and went on a few tours.

My lord, I forgot how much I loved New York theater, and I was so glad to share the experience with young student Andrew. We parted ways for a few days while he visited his married brother near Charlotte, and I visited William and Betsy Hillhouse, a cousin who lived nearby in New Bern, North Carolina. Then we traveled on to Vero Beach, Florida, to visit my brother John who was nine years younger than me.

I think I mentioned it before, but my brother John, just like our Dad, worked in management for the Great Atlantic & Pacific Tea Company (the A&P) in New York City for 34 years. He went on to work 15 years for the Marble Collegiate Church, a huge stone edifice in Midtown Manhattan. He retired in 1995 to Vero Beach where he'd been active in the Community Church there since 1973. He quit drinking in 1972, just as I did in 1981, and he became involved in the National Council on Alcoholism.

Without mentioning my brother's name, Dr. Arthur Caliandro, the former head of the Marble Collegiate Church, wrote an article in August 2011 in which he told of a gay employee coming to him for counsel. That gay employee was my brother John. He shared his anger and confusion with Dr. Caliandro, about how difficult it was for him to live up to our Dad's ideals of what an All-American male should be. Dr. Caliandro wrote about how this visit by my brother John changed forever the way he viewed the gay community.

When we were growing up, I secretly wondered if John was gay. When I came back after WWII in 1946, I moved in with my parents briefly in Buffalo before I headed to New York City. I was sipping a beer at the Statler Hotel bar talking to a guy that I happened to know was gay. In walked my 15-year-old brother John. He said hello to me and also "hello" to the fellow I was talking to—like they were old friends.

John turned to me, "See ya later, Fred."

Just like that, he and my gay friend walked off. That's when I knew for certain John was gay, but that was something no one talked about back then, definitely a taboo subject in our home.

I felt bad for John, not knowing how he would make it in the world, but not during my trip to the east coast and Vero Beach in 2004. We shared lots of memories. On my flight with my PLNU student Andrew back to San Diego, I realized how truly happy John was. No more drinking. No more hiding his truth—he was able to finally live his life in the open and on his terms.

In the year Martha Stewart was sentenced to prison, and gay marriage was legalized in Massachusetts, my brother and I developed a deeper relationship.

* * *

My retirement, my new roof and windows, and my new kitchen fared well in 2005 while Hurricane Katrina destroyed the Gulf Coast, and Arthur Miller and Johnny Carson died. With some of the money from my sister's estate, in early Fall 2006, I flew to New York City for two weeks to take in some new shows and visit old friends. And take in some shows I did—16 altogether—to do that I attended matinees and evening performances.

I stayed at the Crown Plaza Hotel in Times Square where 60 years before I frequented all the clubs, their unending entertainment, and drinking my share of cold 50-cent Millers in frosted glasses. Weeks before my trip, I saw an exposé on TV about a bed bug problem in my hotel—but it was all cleaned up before I arrived.

To finish off my trip, I took in a tour of Radio City Music Hall and visited with friends and a few relatives. That year, *Jersey Boys* won the Tony for Best Musical. I saw it in San Diego at the La Jolla Playhouse where Des MacAnuff brought it to life—long before it went to New York. Over the years, I've seen it five times and even got to know the star of the show, John Lloyd Young.

Here I was at 85 years old, and my passion for live theater was stronger than ever—but I couldn't help but wonder how many more times I would be capable of taking a trip like this again.

26

Al Gore won the Nobel Peace Prize in 2007 for his work on Climate Change, and Deborah Kerr passed away. She was most famous for her love scene in *From Here to Eternity*, passionately kissing Burt Lancaster while Hawaiian waves crashed into them on the sand. I was in Hawaii only twice, during WWII on my way to Okinawa and coming back, and never experienced anything like that. I liked her acting in *Tea & Sympathy*, then she was with Yul Brenner in *The King and I*, and *An Affair to Remember* with Cary Grant. Such grace and beauty. As you can tell, I watch a lot of Turner Classic Movies on TV.

The year passed by extra slow without any pets or work, but I kept myself occupied with my garden, taking in some theater now and then, and my PLNU students who would drive me on my errands and appointments each week. I'm glad UBER wasn't around then, because I really enjoyed their company. There's nothing quite like young students with all their energy, and their lives ahead of them—their perspectives so fresh.

One of my favorites times is when they were studying something historical in school, like an event from the last century, and they would ask me about my firsthand experience. "What was it like, Fred?"

"Well…," I'd begin, and go on and on, dipping into my memories, wading through the years, going to my files for some show-and-tell.

* * *

There were many highs, and only one low in 2008—the low being surgery in July. Seems my gallbladder had enough of the fat I kept pushing through it, so it pushed back with a bunch of gallstones. Recovery was pretty quick—they used something called a laparoscopic procedure where they blew up my abdomen like a beach ball and put in a couple of probes to do their business. I thought I'd end up with scars like I got from my hip and knee replacements, but no, just a few stitches. However, my arm pit hair and eyelashes disappeared.

I questioned my doctor during a follow-up visit. "Can you explain this?" I asked, raising up my shirt and also pointing to my eyebrows.

"Hmm," he said as he poked and prodded. "Mr. Hillhouse, you've stumped me. I have no idea why this happened."

To celebrate my renewed health, I took a trip to Las Vegas where I stayed at the Tropicana Hotel (their Monte Cristo sandwiches in the Palm Room are incredible). I had a three-day coupon for the hotel from the roofing contractor who took care of my home—so I turned it into a week. Brent Littlefield and his wife lived in Las Vegas (I met his father when I was with the San Francisco Giants), so I took them to see *O*, a Cirque de Soleil show. Brent was a chef at one of the bigger hotels, I forget which one. I caught four other shows during my trip, did several tours, and lots of gambling—all on slots, three thousand dollars' worth, which I budgeted.

Cirque de Soleil's O

A deep sadness struck me on September 2, 2008, when I received a call from my niece, Susan Beach. My grand-nephew Brandon died in a hit-and-run on his bicycle. What a sweet young man, and passing away at only 27 years old. He worked with his father Guy on his painting business, even working on some rooms in my home.

I have a framed treasured copy of a story Brandon wrote about me when he was in the third grade.

Brandon Beach – October 18, 1989
One day a person told me that there was an earthquake in San Francisco. My uncle went to San Francisco so I hope is all right. I hoped not a lot of people would die. I prayed for everybody in San Francisco. The World Series was canceled, so the people were scared when it happened. I can't wait until my uncle comes home. Then I will be so happy.

The End

Brandon Beach
June 15, 1981 to September 2, 2008

In early November, I was overwhelmed when a man named Barack Obama was elected president, beating out an old white Vietnam war hero from Arizona and his nutty female running mate from Alaska. I remembered in 1960 thinking how a Catholic could ever become president—then there was JFK. I never, and I mean never, believed this country would elect a black man into office during my lifetime. I'm proud to say I voted for him in 2008 and again in 2012.

I called up my brother John when the California Supreme Court ruled in 2008 that same sex couples could marry. He was elated, but shared his disappointment in Florida's laws where he lived. It would take seven more years before that would change in 2015, not that John was in the marrying mood at 77 years old.

I ended the year by sending out my annual custom Christmas Cards to both a growing and shrinking list of addressees—shrinking because of the people I was outliving at 87 years old, and growing because of the number of politicians and celebrities I added to my holiday wishes, the Pope included. If Paul Newman and Cyd Charisse had been on my list, I would have had to remove them, because they passed away that year.

* * *

The next year started with an airliner full of passengers landing in the middle of the cold Hudson River in New York City—and no one died. I was riveted to CNN as they covered some good news for once. Speaking of New York City, in

March 2009, Bernie Maddoff was officially charged with bilking hundreds of people out of $50 billion. *Fifty billion dollars.* In all the bookkeeping I did in my careers, 10 years with Buffalo Solvents and Chemicals, 18 years with the San Francisco Giants, and 21 years with the New Frontier Trading Corporation, I never saw more than $10 million in a bank account. I just couldn't imagine how someone could take $50 billion from investors.

The news was constantly filled with the stock market crashing, housing falling apart, huge businesses on the brink of bankruptcy, and a Swine Flu outbreak in Mexico. Two thousand nine started out a very crazy year, and I watched it all on TV, enjoying my discussions with my PLNU students.

In June, Michael Jackson died. Walter Cronkite passed away the next month—what a remarkable voice and delivery of the news, called "the most trusted man in America" at one time. Aside from my favorite TV shows, I watched a lot of CNN for Obama's inauguration, and the retrospectives of the celebrities who passed away. Then there was the growing threat of more terrorism, and our financial collapse—vacant homes sprouting up everywhere, and the value of real estate in a free fall. A tumultuous year all around—2010 had to be better.

* * *

In the Spring of 2010, I flew to San Francisco for a one-week visit with friends and saw two shows. At 88-years-old, I took advantage of wheelchairs at the airports, but stood on my own two feet everywhere else I went. On my way to the airport to head back to San Diego, I asked the cabbie to pass by my old home that I bought for $30,000 in 1971 and sold in 1976 for $64,000—it still looked the same. When I got home, my PLNU student checked on the internet for information on the first house I ever lived in. It had just sold for $900,000!

A month before the San Francisco Giants beat the Texas Rangers to win the World Series, Tony Curtis died—I didn't think he was that old, but he was three years younger than me. That made me feel older than I ever had.

* * *

In February 2011, I celebrated my brother Andy's 91st birthday, his third wife Eva preparing a delicious meal, and his daughter Susan coming down from Murrieta with a cake. Andy married three times—amazing that he was the only one of my siblings to marry, John not able to until same-sex laws were changed, and my sister Nancy never found the right guy, or enjoyed partying too much. Me? Maybe I was just too selfish, spending so much of my free time enjoying live entertainment and buying performers drinks.

I looked around the birthday table at Andy and it hit me— how old and tired he looked. It was as if the last 40 years of his life caught up to him all at once. Two months later, it did when he was taken to the hospital with chest pains. His daughter Susan from Murrieta rushed down to stay with him, and his other daughter Sara flew in from Paris after the doctor said it didn't look so good. I had a chance to say goodbye to Andy in the quiet way only two brothers from New York could—spaces between words filled with so much unsaid emotion.

He was buried at the Miramar National Cemetery in a military ceremony—the bugler playing *Taps*, the folded flag from his casket handed to his wife by a kneeling Marine. I fought off tears. About 35 people attended the outdoor service, a cool but typically sunny San Diego day. Some nice words were spoken, but not by me—I was never one to do any public speaking.

I found myself taking in the ceremony and thinking that half of the Andrew Hillhouse Sr. and Ednah Hillhouse children were gone—John and I were all that was left. I wondered which one of us would go next.

In the year Prince William married, Osama bin Laden was killed, and the *King's Speech* won the Oscar for Best Picture, my brother Andy's casket was lowered into a hole in the ground.

That November, I received my first birthday card from the White House, President Barack Obama and his wife Michele sending me greetings. Apparently, if you sign up for it, anyone over 90 years old can get a birthday card from the president every year. That was a nice touch, capping off a year of deep loss.

27

I kept seeing Fred Thompson on TV, you know, the actor who played hard-boiled district attorney Arthur Branch on *Law and Order*, and went on to became a US Senator from Tennessee? Well, he'd go on about how a reverse mortgage was a great way for an aging American to get money out of their home—a monthly payment *to you*, and you could live in your home for free. I signed up.

With some cash from that, 2012 started out with a little project that took a full month to finish—my bathroom got a complete remodel. A new vanity, john, and shower really brightened up my single bath home.

As usual, three times a week, a Point Loma Nazarene student would come by to take me on errands and appointments. My doctors kept telling me I was doing remarkably well for a 90-year-old man with two fake hips, a fake knee, missing gallstones, and a down-sized prostate—but I was feeling all of it.

A few spots showed up on my head. "Pre-cancerous," the dermatologist said as she froze them—the discoloration and scabs taking nearly a month to heal.

Once that was out of the way, the pattern of my life settled back in and became more predictable. I liked it that way.

* * *

Sherlock Holmes had his Professor Moriarty, Superman his kryptonite, but my nemesis ended up being a garden hose. On a sunny April 2012 day in San Diego, I futzed about my backyard as usual—pulling some weeds here, trimming a bush there, watering plants. I was wearing a pair of brown Crocks, the rubberized slipper-type shoes with the big holes in them that look like a cross between Swiss cheese and the wooden clogs you see in Hans Christian Anderson stories.

I turned to take a few steps to the trash can to deposit a handful of leaves—then it happened. My Crocks got tangled in the garden hose and I toppled forward. My forehead hit the edge of a bench with a dull thud. I reached for my cell phone, flipped it open, and blinked away the blood pouring down from my forehead, and dialed 9-1-1. Then I passed out.

* * *

I have no memory of the next two months—none at all. I guess that's what happens when you suffer a severe concussion and almost break your neck. Apparently, after I dialed, I tried to stand up and fell back, smashing the back of my head on the concrete patio.

Losing my memory was by far the strangest thing that ever happened to me. I have excellent recall and an even better filing system. If you want to know the last inoculation I received in the Navy, or what my grades were in seventh grade, all I have to do is go to a spiral tablet, which tells me which cupboard to look in, go to that cupboard and retrieve the box where the document resides. Simple. But this, this no memory for two months unnerved me and had me stumped—somewhat afraid.

Coming out of my "cloud," the first thing I saw was Drew Carey on TV on *The Price is Right*, teasing a cute brunette who guessed the right price of a blender and was on her way to some kind of showcase. I tried to crane my neck to look outside the window, but I couldn't.

A dreadful thought flashed across my mind, *I am paralyzed.*

I lifted my right hand in front of my eyes and wiggled my fingers. I glanced down to discover I was in an upper body brace that disallowed neck movement. I noticed a red button with a gray cord wrapped around the rail of my bed. I pushed it. Moments later, a smiling red-headed nurse, in a crisp white uniform stepped into the room.

"Well, Mr. Hillhouse, how are we doing today?"

I smacked my lips and tried to form words, but my throat was dry and all that came out was a soft wheeze.

"By the way, I'm Donna. Let me get you some water," she guessed, then disappeared from my view to the right. I heard her set down a plastic cup and pour water. She reappeared and held a straw up to my mouth. "Slowly now. No big gulps."

You hear stories of people stranded in the desert and all they want is a simple drink of water—and how they will do anything for it. That's how I felt. I sucked hard on that straw and took in too much at once, some going down my wind pipe. She pulled the straw away as I began to hack.

"I told you, slowly." Her brow furrowed in concern, she waited until my cough eased.

"Where am I?" I croaked.

She reached down and took hold of my hand, speaking slowly, "You had a fall and hurt your neck, that's why the upper-body brace."

"When—when did it happen?"

"After going to the hospital, you've been with us about two months now."

"But where is this?"

"You're in the Mission Hills Therapy Center."

I tried to shake my head and let out a long sigh. "Really?"

* * *

The first thing that flooded my mind was my garden and all my monthly payments, but Scott, one of my Point Loma Nazarene students and his mother, came over once to take care of my yard. My student caregiver, Gregory, picked up my mail and brought it to me. It was great having them take care of that—relieving my worry.

My nieces, Susan and Sarah, spoke to my doctor to learn I fractured the fifth vertebrae in my neck during my fall. "Your uncle will never be able to live alone again."

When I heard that, I was more determined than ever to make a full recovery.

* * *

I shared my room with Ronaldo, a 65-year-old Hispanic Don Juan. I called him that because I woke up more than once in the middle of the night to rhythmic low thumping and groaning sounds. I saw shadows on the curtain separating our beds, and guessed a nurse was having sex with him. If I could have, I would have reached over and yanked the curtain aside to get an eyeful.

* * *

My biggest challenge was to teach my atrophied muscles how to do everything again, even something as simple as using a fork. But it was walking that got to me. Gripping onto gray rubber handles, I shuffled my feet down polished linoleum corridors—using a walker, with a physical therapist at my side, his hand on the belt at my lower back. It was almost as embarrassing as it was frustrating.

In June, I came home for two days accompanied by a nurse. It was incredible to be back in my place, surrounded by my things. However, I had a setback when I fainted during a doctor's appointment. So, it was back to the hospital for a week—then to a care home run by a Filipino couple. The husband and wife each had jobs. She worked as a nurse at night, and the husband at some factory during the day. Three older women were there as well, recovering from surgery or strokes. One couldn't talk, one couldn't hear, and the other was anti-social, staying in her room most of the time. As you can tell, that wasn't too much fun.

The Filipino couple helped me over the next six months with everything from preparing meals (canned corned served at supper every day), and taking me to doctor's appointments. I paid for it all. $2,500 a month, plus $25 an hour when they drove me to appointments. They were pleasant enough, but I could tell they were doing it all for the money. I felt helpless, my independence gone just because I tripped on a garden hose.

In August, maybe because of all the stress, my heart acted up. I found myself having spells where I felt a weight press on my chest. After a raft of tests, Dr. Charles Athill installed a pacemaker in my chest. Now I really felt like a bionic man.

October brought me smiles when my San Francisco Giants beat the Detroit Tigers to win the World Series. My Filipino caregivers couldn't quite understand how I could get excited about such a boring game.

"Mr. Fred, why do you like the baseball so much, Nancy asked?" (I was supposed to pronounce her real name Nahn-SAY, but I just couldn't bring myself to do it).

"I don't really, but since I worked for the San Francisco Giants for eighteen years, it's fun to root for them. Besides, what else is there to do?"

Following my 91st birthday on November 5, 2012, I got a lot of pleasure out of voting for Obama again and watching him defeat Mitt Romney. Soon after, I received my birthday card from President Obama and showed it to my caregivers. They were impressed.

"Mr. Fred, you know president?"

"That's not all. If you ever visit me in my home, I can show you autographs of famous Broadway stars and more."

I felt real bad I didn't send out my annual custom Christmas cards in 2012, especially when so many were sent to me. But I spent the year recovering from a broken neck and amnesia, the best and worst excuse I could have—I wouldn't wish that on anyone.

During my stay in the recovery home, twice they took us for an outing to the Hometown Buffet. They moved us around like we were a bunch of invalids, making sure everyone got their food on trays and brought them to the table.

After sixth months, I escaped (it felt that way) from the Filipinos. In early December, I hired a caregiver to drive me home. There were no sad goodbyes when I left the recovery home, especially with three old women who were no company at all.

The year ended on such a sad note. Twenty children from Sandy Hook Elementary School in Connecticut were killed by a crazed gunman. That's all the newscasters talked about, voices beseeching for some kind of change to our laws to prevent this kind of tragedy from happening again. Ninety-one years on the planet and I was so saddened that this could happen here, in my America.

28

I was more than glad to be back in my place, but I needed a walker to navigate every step I took—something I wasn't too happy about. I contacted Point Loma Nazarene and they sent over another student who began coming by two or three times a week for errands and doctors' appointments. God, it was nice to be home and away from that rehab house.

Ruth Kreidt, the widow living across the street, came over to see how I was doing. She was in my back yard the afternoon of my garden-hose accident and felt so bad she didn't help— but she didn't know anything about it. We promised then and there, that each morning around nine a.m. we would call to see how we each were doing. This was how a typical conversation would go.

"How are you doing this morning, Fred?"

"Just fine, Ruth. A little stiff getting out of bed, but that's just the way it is, isn't it?"

She'd laugh. "Yes. Chilly today, and it looks like we might get some rain."

"That'd be nice. Then I won't have to water my plants."

"Yes, you and your plants."

"Ruth, I got some new magazines in. If you want to come by sometime, maybe later, I'll trade you."

"Thank you, Fred. I'll call before I drop by."

It was good to know someone cared with a call every morning, verifying that we made it through another night—and we were still alive.

* * *

I made myself a quiet Christmas dinner, a turkey sandwich with cranberry sauce, and got calls from my two nieces, and my brother John, wishing me their best.

On New Year's Eve, I watched the ball drop at nine p.m. on CNN after their remembrance and memorials from 2012. Some of the names caught me by surprise—Neil Armstrong, Dick Clark, Andy Williams, and Etta James—all gone. I couldn't help but wonder when my time would come.

I shuffled off to bed early New Year's Eve, hoping, no, praying that 2013 would be a better year. It had to be. "I'm too old for this shit," I mumbled to myself as I fell asleep.

* * *

My life fell back into its old pattern from before my accident—but much slower because of my walker. Go to bed at nine-thirty every night, wake up around six, fix a light breakfast, then catch up on the news from CNN—and call Ruth at nine a.m. When the weather was nice, I'd head out to my back yard for little tasks to straighten things up, maybe repot a plant, pick up some leaves—but never trip on a hose again. It was slow going with my walker.

I grabbed snacks here and there during the day, usually a cookie or two—my sweet tooth as strong as ever. Pick up a rerun of *Judge Judy* in the morning, have some lunch followed by the *Bold & Beautiful*, and *The Young & The Restless*. Take a little cat nap. *Judge Judy* again later in the afternoon. Dinner, then channel surf the rest of the evening unless *Dancing with the Stars* or *Big Brother* was on.

I know, not very exciting. What I really looked forward to most was phone calls from friends and what remained of my family—my brother John and my two nieces. Susan and her husband Guy lived in Murrieta, California, about an hour and a half away by car, Sara in Paris, and John in Florida.

Every time the phone rang, I got to it as fast as I could, made sure to mute the TV, and take out my hearing aid so I could the hear the caller. Problem was, five calls a day were from telemarketers, and most of the time I didn't understand them. They talked too fast and with strange accents, I just hung up. I learned not to answer.

I curtailed a very special activity because of my walker—going to live theater. No more plays or musicals. I remember how I felt looking at people being wheeled into an auditorium, ushers making a fuss over them, a blanket over their weak legs. I couldn't stand the thought of someone seeing me that way.

MY HOMES I REMEMBER

SYRACUSE, NEW YORK *1930*

UTICA, NEW YORK *1939*

CLINTON, NEW YORK *1940*

U.S. NAVY – LST 1071 *1942*

AT CHRISTMAS TIME

BUFFALO, NEW YORK *1946*

KENMORE, NEW YORK *1948*

SAN FRANCISCO, CALIFORNIA *1958*

SAN DIEGO, CALIFORNIA *1976*

Inside of 2013 Christmas Card

In early 2013, I began to plan my custom Christmas cards. Since I missed the previous year, this one needed to be extra special. I spent days going through old photos and came up with a fun idea—to put pictures of all the homes I ever lived in along with the city and the year. That included childhood homes to my current one where I've lived since 1976.

For the eight months while I was in the hospital, rehab, and the Filipino care home, my participation in the Publishers Clearing House contests lagged. I made up for it though, buying the cheapest stuff they offered—all designed to give me better odds to win (even though it stated it didn't). A super bright flashlight, kitchen gadgets, and a tangle-free garden hose were some of what I ordered. I got a call from one of their representatives to ask how old I was. When I told him 91, he assured me that my prize of $5,000 a week for life could be transferred to anyone else—should I win. That gave me hope— maybe I was closing in on the grand prize.

On February 3, 2013, I watched my San Francisco 49ers lose to the Ravens in the Super Bowl, two brothers coaching the opposing teams. After that, life plodded along, assisted by my walker, and my university student stopping by. Roger Ebert died in early April, and then a few weeks later during the Boston Marathon there was that bombing. What a sad world this had become.

The day before Thanksgiving, I sent out my Christmas cards to addressees out of town—the others going out on December first, my mailing grown to 200 by then. Over the next month, I received return cards, letters, and phone calls filling me with unending joy and entertainment, people remarking how unique my homes were, especially the LST 1071 Navy ship I lived on during WWII. I placed all their cards and letters in return in a large basket on my coffee table. Every few days or so, I sat down to look through them and relive the smiles I felt when I first opened them. I usually kept the Obamas' card on top to show to visitors.

The year finished and blended into 2014 without much notice. The husbands of a few more couples I knew passed away. Besides Ruth from a cross the street, I now had four other widows who kept in touch with me—mostly phone calls with friendly greetings.

* * *

My Christmas card list for 2014 grew and my theme for my custom card that year was about my membership in The Mayflower Society, something of great pride to me. I mentioned before that I'm a 10th-generation descendant of William Bradford, the first governor and historian of the Plymouth Colony. He wrote journals of all their goings-on for their first 31 years. The response from my friends was fantastic, letters, cards, phone calls. That kept me busy and reminded me that there was something special about my being here in this world.

* * *

Two things excited me in 2015—getting an article about me placed in the San Diego Union-Tribune, and hiring someone to help me write my memoir.

The UT article was titled, "Want to clear your conscience?" I contacted the paper and they liked my story idea, having a reporter interview me over the phone. It was published on the 24th anniversary of my precious VW Bug being stolen from my driveway. I hoped someone might come forward and that I could get closure on that sad event in my life. The article got some big laughs from the five widows, my Point Loma Nazarene students, and my family. No closure though.

I was forever being told what a long and amazing life I lived. So, under the urging of students, caregivers, friends, and family, I hired an author to begin writing my life story. I figured the cost into my monthly budget, as you'd expect, and I met with her every other week to write about my life. She was amazed at the documents I provided her which she drew from to scribe dozens of pages.

I designed my new Christmas cards for 2015, featuring a fresh photo of me standing without my walker, and a list of all the physical changes and ailments I went through in my life. There were the little things like gray and thinning hair, glasses, hearing aids, and support hose. A few diseases and conditions that plagued me in my later years included chronic venous insufficiency, shingles, and arthritis. The operations my aging body undertook included two hip replacements, right knee replacement, prostate surgery, gall bladder surgery, and a pacemaker.

In early 2016, my ghostwriter moved away and I was at a loss of what to do next. Matt, my current Point Loma Nazarene student, suggested we put an ad on Craigslist to find a new writer.

"What's a Craigslist?" I asked.

His broad smile showed me how out of touch I was with technology, but he explained, "It's a place where you can put an ad online for free to either sell something or find some help."

"Online?"

"Yes, on the internet."

"Oh, the internet. What's that like?"

"You'll see how easy it is."

He took out his computer, wrote up the ad, and he "posted" my ad online, with him listed as the contact. A day later, he called to let me know that six people already responded. The following day, there were another ten.

"Should we interview them all?" I asked, overwhelmed by the task at hand.

"No, I'll sort through them, pick a few who look good, then let's meet them."

"Oh my, that sounds like lots of work, Matt."

"Not really, Fred. It'll be fun."

Within a week, in March 2016, I chose my new ghostwriter. You never know how you're going to work with someone on an important project. I hoped he'd be someone who gets to know me well enough to capture my voice to tell my story. I think he did a great job.

Besides working with my new ghostwriter on my book during 2016, I designed my custom Christmas cards and increased my mailing list to 242—adding the Queen of England, Prince Harry, the Pope, and a few other notables. That year's card featured a new photo of me in my backyard near my plants. Then I added pictures from my life—at 22 during my first year in the Navy, at 40 when I worked for the San Francisco Giants, and at 50, still with the Giants, but shortly after I bought my first home.

On January 1, 2017, I woke, and as usual, went through my usual routine, but when I went to get my newspaper at 7:30, it wasn't there. I checked with my neighbors and they hadn't received theirs either. I called the delivery service a few times, left messages, and told Ruth I was on top of it, she was missing her paper as well. At 9:00 a.m. it arrived. I hoped it wasn't an omen of the year to come.

29

A Christmas card photo of my niece Sara and her family in France.

Sara and her husband Francois live near Paris and spend summers in Connecticut. Recently I learned how to use my computer and now can talk to her online and even send and receive emails. I have a feeling my typewriter may be seeing the end of its days.

Here's a quick update on what's going on with their five children:

William, 28, works in New York City in sales for a software products company.

Henry, 26, works in Boston at a private equity firm.

Joseph, 22, is in college in Lille, France, studying computer and software engineering.

James, 19, is at Brown University, studying history and political science.

Eliza, 15, is in 10th grand in high school in France.

Of note, Eliza, Joseph, and James sang in the Children's Chorus at the Paris National Opera. Joseph also traveled for four years to Egypt, Jordan, and Syria. James spent two years between Japan and the US, while Eliza was in Paris for two years.

* * *

In June 2017, at 95 years old, as I reflect on my life, a few things stand out.

I've attended four funerals, my grandmother's when I was in my late teens—we went out to a number of New York City clubs afterward to celebrate. Then there were the funerals of my parents, and my brother Andy. There was no funeral or ceremony I remember for Joanne, my baby sister who died at two months old, born with encephalitis in 1929 when I was eight and living in Syracuse—and something a family like ours never discussed. I missed my sister Nancy's funeral because my health was so poor, but say a silent thanks to her each time I hear rain pounding on my roof or look out my double-paned windows at my back yard—her estate leaving me enough money for that and a few trips.

The saddest of the deaths was that of my great nephew Brandon, my niece Susan and Guy's son. One minute he was riding a bicycle down a quiet street, and the next thing you know, he's found in a ditch, the victim of a hit-and-run. So much life ahead of him, and such a handsome fine young man.

I've seen more than 500 plays and musicals and can show you the playbills, many autographed, from all of them.

I have everything I need—a home, garden, and friends. I have help to tend to my home and yard, a caregiver for medical needs and appointments, and I'm grateful to the students who take me on errands. I also have very good medical insurance.

I've enjoyed my life, as simple and uneventful as it might seem to some. I never minded not marrying or being by myself most of the time, although I've had spells of loneliness. The past 35 years of my life, since I stopped drinking in 1981, have left me more lonely without the fun and camaraderie I shared with bar patrons as we watched live entertainment and toasted the performers every Friday and Saturday night.

I have no idea what awaits me when I die. I was baptized at 11 years old, but never took to it or any religion during my life. I'm not afraid of death—I just don't want to suffer when I go. That's not much to ask.

Now, I think I'll go type a letter to Hillary Clinton. I have a computer I'm learning to use, but I think I'll just clack it out on my electric typewriter. I have her mailing address. I suppose one of her staff will open it and toss it aside with the hundreds of other letters she receives. I want her to know that I admire her for running for president, and that she would have been so much better than "the Donald."

Like I've done all my life with every document, I will make a copy of that letter, place it a folder, put that in a box, place the box back on a shelf, log its location, and be able to quickly retrieve it—should anyone ask.

If you perchance call me and ask, "How are you doing, Fred?"—be ready for my standard answer. My nieces have heard it many times and it always gives them a laugh.

"As good as can be expected under the conditions that prevail."

Thank you for listening.

51176283R00146

Made in the USA
San Bernardino, CA
14 July 2017